I'LL NEVER GROW UP!

THE BARE NECESSITIES OF PLANNING YOUR DISNEYLAND VACATION

RENEE TSANG

Modern Bluebell Press

First edition

Published by Modern Bluebell Press 2019 (updated 2021)

ISBN (print): 978-1-9992379-0-5

ISBN (ebook): 978-1-9992379-1-2

Cover Design: 100Covers

Editor: Catherine Turner

Photographer: Sarazin Photography

"The magic is as wide as a smile and as narrow as a wink,

loud as laughter and quiet as a tear,

tall as a tale and deep as emotion.

So strong, it can lift the spirit.

So gentle, it can touch the heart.

It is the magic that begins the happily ever after."

- Walt Disney

CONTENTS

LEGAL NOTICE & DISCLAIMER

This is an unofficial book detailing personal experiences at Disneyland and recommendations for others who are planning to visit. This book does not imply any endorsement, affiliation or association with any Disney company in any way. This book is independently produced and created by the author.

The author, the book and its publisher are not affiliated with Disney, The Walt Disney Company, The Disneyland Resort or any of its affiliates. All rides and attraction names are property of or copyright of the Walt Disney Company, and we do not claim any copyright over any of the rides, movies or attractions mentioned in this guide. All content in the book are the intellectual property of The Walt Disney Company and trademarked as such. This includes all of the characters, trademarks, images, wardrobe or any other identifiable marks that are the property of their Disney owners. All trademarks belong to their respective owners.

This book is presented solely as a guide for educational and entertainment purposes. The author and publisher are not offering it as any professional advice. While best efforts have been made in preparing this book, the author and publisher make no representations or warranties of any kind and assume no liabilities of any kind with respect to the accuracy or completeness of the contents.

ALL ABOUT ME

1

INTRODUCTION

I am writing this book as a way to share my experiences, in the same way that I decided to start a travel business for myself almost six years ago. I had initially started my blog, (www.lifeistooshort-tostayhome.com) as an outlet for me to share my experiences as a travel consultant and my adventures in travelling.

"Life is too short to stay home" became my vision of how life should be. Because home is where the heart is, and for me, the feeling of "home" doesn't have to be tied to a physical place.

My life has always felt somewhat nomadic. I grew up in a small town in Saskatchewan where the summers were long, and there was little to do. So every summer, my dad would take at least three weeks off work and take us on road trips across Canada and the U.S.A in our brown Dodge van (We put a lot of mileage on that van!). A couple of those years, we even travelled overseas and spent our summers in Hong Kong and Taiwan living like locals for a couple of months.

Many of my milestone childhood events and memories are rooted in travel experiences. But it wasn't until after I became a parent and had two kids of my own, that my passion for travel was re-ignited, and I wondered to myself *"Why I haven't I travelled in so long?"*

I went into the travel industry as a hobby to explore opportunities to travel. I enjoy planning travel and want to give my kids the same type of travel opportunities my parents gave me. And I love being in the travel industry! There are so many training opportunities to discover new destinations. The inspiration to explore the world and enrich life experiences through travel became an important beacon of light.

My mother unexpectedly passed away less than a year after I started my travel business. Gone were all the lofty dreams of memorable family vacations with my kids and their grandparents. Memories like those I have from my childhood, travelling with my parents and my grandmas.

After my mother's passing, my dad and I spent a lot of time going through her belongings - a lifetime of memories, trimming things down to the bare necessities. He was downsizing from a large family home of seven (I'm the oldest of five children) to a small condo for two in another province two hours away. They had planned on moving to Vancouver after my dad retired, an easy launchpad to travel and explore the world - the perfect retirement plan.

Alas, things in life don't always go according to plan. And going through a house filled with over 30 years of stuff collected from our childhood was an emotionally exhausting endeavour.

Drowning in the sadness of my mother's passing also fuelled me with the need to really live and enjoy life in the present. Because you don't know how precious certain treasures are until they are gone and all you are left with are memories. And suddenly, when all you have are memories, it becomes that much more important to have unforgettable ones, and ones rooted in as much joy and happiness as possible.

The whole process of grief and going through a lifetime of stuff made me really sit back and think about my life, and the legacy I want to leave for my kids. It is certainly not material things. The last thing I want for my kids is to go through the arduous task of sifting through a lifetime of my belongings.

Instead, I want my legacy for them to be our experiences of our life together, and the memories of the adventures we have.

I decided that

I will not live in sadness.

I will not let life events define me and how I choose to live.

I choose joy and happiness.

And I am in complete control of my life and how I choose to live it.

It was then I decided to downsize now, when my kids are still young. To live within our means, without any extraneous stuff. We got rid of the excess and started to live a somewhat minimalist lifestyle, to what we considered "the bare necessities".

We spend all our time and energy on experiences. It is just the three of us, and I am determined to give them the best childhood I can with the means available to me, especially as a single parent.

I do not want to deprive them of any available opportunities and experiences if I have the means to make it possible. In an industry full of opportunity and adventure, why not take the opportunities I have to give them the most amazing vacation experiences, and memories that they will always cherish?

As parents, don't we want the best for our children and to provide as much as we can for them?

Why wait until someday?

My mother's death reminded me that tomorrow is never guaranteed. We had all these grand plans, and they were never realized because she had an incurable brain tumour. But yet, it didn't stop her from living her life to the fullest and experiencing travel and life adventures.

Life is just one big journey, and I certainly don't have it all figured out yet. But the process has taught me to enjoy the journey, to fully enjoy the present while creating our future.

"We keep moving forward, opening new doors, and doing new things, because we're curious and curiosity keeps leading us down new paths."
Walt Disney

2

WHAT'S IT ALL ABOUT

This guide is a collection of everything you need to know about planning a trip to Disneyland. As a College of Disney Knowledge Graduate though my education as a Disney travel agent, I've utilized the resources available to me to put this book together. I've also drawn on my own personal experiences in planning my own trips as well as client trips, to stay updated with all the latest happenings in Disneyland.

The thing is, while you can know all the ins and outs of Disney vacation planning, it can easily change as Disney is constantly changing policies, improving things, and continuing to evolve and add new experiences for you to enjoy.

It did occur to me that it might not be in my best interest to write a book about a topic that can easily change (and does easily change!), but at the same time, the magical experience of Disney and what it offers will never change.

So because of that, the inspiration to visit time and time again is what drives me to stay immersed in the magical world of Disney and the never-ending wonder that it continues to be.

And, that's one of the things I love **most** about Disney. It evolves and changes with the times. Same, but different. Familiar, yet new. It's why Disney fans return to Disneyland and never tire of the place - of the magic. Memories unchanged in spirit and heart. It stays current by adding new attractions, shows, and entertainment, but the classics endure. The stories are timeless, and the magic and fun will always remain.

> *"Disneyland will never be completed.*
> *It will continue to grow as long as there is imagination left in the world."*
> *Walt Disney*

While you can read this book in sequential order from front to back, it's also designed to give you the information you need quickly so that you don't have to read it in full to find your answer. You can easily hop around sections to read what is relevant to you.

Disney planning is overwhelming. There is a lot to discover. And there's only so much information your brain can handle at one time. If you're not familiar with Disney at all, then the mere thought of planning a Disneyland vacation can send your head spinning into a whirlwind and make you want to give up.

So I get it. My brain works much in the same way where I have a jumble of thoughts all over the place and I just have to get the information out. That's kind of how this book started - a collection of useful information and tidbits that will come in handy in different situations and detailed answers to some of the most commonly asked questions my clients had. There is a lot of information about Disneyland available, but I've highlighted the most important bits to help you plan your visit and make it a little bit easier for you.

If it is your first time planning a trip to Disneyland, I highly recommend working with a Disney Vacation Specialist to help you navigate through some of the details that are specific to planning a

Disney vacation. Half the fun is in the planning, and a Disney Vacation Specialist will help you with the magical details from the start through to your travel. This book is focused on Disneyland in Anaheim, California, as a trip to Walt Disney World in Orlando is a separate type of vacation altogether and deserves its own edition.

I start with Disneyland because it is where all Disney vacations begin. Whether you visit Walt Disney World in Orlando, Disneyland Paris, Hong Kong Disneyland, Shanghai Disneyland, Tokyo Disneyland, Disney Cruise Line, Adventures by Disney, or Aulani, A Disney Resort & Spa in Ko Olina, Hawaii, the Disney experience stems from the original Disneyland Park in Anaheim. The original park was created by Walt Disney, the man behind the mouse, whose legacy is carried on throughout the world in celebrating the magic of imagination and unforgettable stories and experiences. Why not start where you can witness his legacy first-hand?

After reading this guide, you will know all the ins and outs of booking a Disneyland vacation, deciding when the best time to travel will be, where to stay, with park tips and strategies depending on how many days you plan on spending at the parks. And while you can plan your own trip after reading this book, I also highly recommend working with a Disney Vacation Specialist, a travel agent that is knowledgeable and specializes in Disney destinations to assist with your plans, and to support a local small business who revels in sharing the magic of Disney with you and your family!

If you would like travel planning assistance to help with booking your Disneyland vacation, you can reach out anytime to work with me!

Website: www.ReneeTsangTravel.com
Blog: www.lifeistooshorttostayhome.com

Facebook/Instagram
@reneetsangtravel

3

I'LL NEVER GROW UP!

My very first trip to Disneyland was when I was eight, but I don't remember much about that trip. This was in the mid-eighties and we drove from Moose Jaw, Saskatchewan, to Los Angeles, California. We have a couple of old photos, but nowhere near as many as what we take for vacation photos nowadays! We travelled each year, so sometimes my childhood travel memories are jumbled together rather than being specific trip memories. But that is also how I remember my childhood; we travelled and went on some pretty memorable road trips, seeing some pretty amazing places along the way, visiting family and friends throughout Canada and the U.S.A.

We did visit Walt Disney World in Orlando a few times throughout my childhood, but it wasn't until my first visit to Disneyland Paris as an adult (and as a parent) that the magical world of Disney really opened my eyes to the whole experience. As much as I enjoyed the experience as an individual, I couldn't help but think how much I wanted to share it with my kids, and I couldn't wait to take them to Disneyland!

During one of my younger self's Walt Disney World trips, our family had gone to Orlando during Christmas break in 1997 , and the crowds were crazy busy. Even then, Magic Kingdom was closed by 9 a.m. on Christmas Day because it had reached crowd capacity at that time. Our family arrived early and made it into Magic Kingdom. My cousins who were travelling with us during that trip did not arrive in time before they closed the parks, so they had to make alternative plans for that day. Crowds were shoulder to shoulder and people were everywhere. There were lines for everything - for rides, for food and for the restrooms. We could never find a place to rest or take a break. And to top it off, we had my 80-something year old grandma and four young kids in four strollers with us as we tried to navigate through crowds as a group of twelve. After that trip, I vowed to myself that I would wait until my kids could walk on their own before I would take them to Disney. I personally did not want to visit Disney with strollers!

My kids were eight and six when we first visited Disneyland, and I felt they were at a perfect age to visit! They were both able to walk, no strollers were needed, and they were ready to tackle the longer park days without needing to take breaks for naps during the day. We could visit the parks, spend as much time as we could fit in that day, and then head back to the hotel when we felt we had exhausted all their energy for the day.

A visit to Disneyland was the perfect place to begin my travel business, and so one of the first tasks I set for myself was to become a Disney Vacation Specialist. Within the first year of my business, we were fortunate enough to visit Aulani, A Disney Resort & Spa in Ko Olina, Hawaii, Disneyland in Anaheim, and take a Disney cruise to Alaska. After that, we were able to visit Disneyland, Walt Disney World in Orlando, and take a Disney cruise to the Bahamas, all within a 10 month time frame. In between all of that, we were fortunate enough to head overseas to Hong Kong to fit in Hong Kong Disneyland!

"It's kind of fun to do the impossible"
Walt Disney

Why not take inspiration from the man himself? What he was able to achieve in his lifetime is nothing short of amazing, awe-inspiring, and full of happiness and joy. This was the legacy he chose, and the imprint he made onto this world is forever etched in all our hearts.

Not that I had any similar grandiose dreams of doing impossible and unachievable things. Content with my life as it was, I did not have any specific aspirations of greatness. But with starting my travel business in 2013, I was looking for the opportunity to travel more with my kids and create some pretty amazing childhood memories along the way.

Travelling was a priority for both my business and for my family. What I didn't realize was that through this process, *my* inner child was also enjoying all the Disney fun! I realized I was enjoying Disney *with* my kids and not just watching them enjoy it for themselves. I was experiencing the joy and magic of Disney through the lens of pure innocence, amazement, and wonder, really enjoying the experience for what it was. That's it. The simplicity of the experience.

As an adult, you will appreciate the level of detail and attention that goes into Disney to make it effortless and intuitive to know what will bring you joy before you even realize you wanted it.

Why Disney?

It's a place of never-ending happiness and joy. It's a place where you can leave the real world behind and return to simpler times where you can focus on the little things and see the joy all around.

I think I enjoy Disney even more as an adult than I did as a child because I can appreciate the attention to detail of each experience, from the vision to execution. How one man's expansive vision to identify the details to create an immersive experience and how that vision is consistently and carefully passed through each Cast Member in the Disney family is beyond comprehension. The assurances of this everlasting legacy are inspiring on so many levels, and you are left in wondrous amazement at how the grand execution of each experience comes together.

Disneyland is the stage where imagination comes alive and dreams come true. And understanding the idea and its journey to what it is today leaves you in awe each time you visit.

ALL ABOUT YOU

WHAT IS THE BEST AGE TO VISIT?

A ll the ages! It's *always* a great time to visit Disney! Why wait to experience Disney when there are magical experiences to be enjoyed at all stages of life?

There is no "perfect" age to visit Disney. It is never too early to introduce your child to Disney. From the moment babies are born, they are introduced to the mass marketing empire of Disney products, and there will be lots of characters, movies, stories and experiences that they will recognize at any age.

Disneyland is a place for all ages, with something for every age and stage of life. There are experiences for each age and the experience is in the moment just as it is meant to be. The magic is just as enthralling for a parent or grandparent as it is for a young child.

Sometimes as adults, we stay so focused on our kids and what they will remember that we forget that Disney is about our memories too! It's easy to have your whole world centred around your child when you first become a parent. It's easy to get caught up in doing everything for your children, to ensure they are having fun, and to make sure they have the best experience possible.

But what about you, the parent? Don't you deserve to have some fun too? What about experiencing the magic through the eyes of your child?

Let's say you decide to take your two-year-old to Disney, and you worry she may not remember anything when she's older. But instead, reframe the decision to think about *your* memories. What about the experience you will have as a parent, to enjoy Disney through your child's eyes?

When you first see the magic of Disney through the eyes of your child, it is a magic that you cannot comprehend until you've experienced it first-hand. And it reminds you of why you do this and why you do it for your child. Why we are parents and why it's all worth it. The magic of Disney is *real.* You will never witness that level of wide-eyed wonder and disbelief through any other experience!

I try not to live my life with any regret. However, I do wish now that I had thought to take my kids to Disneyland when they were younger. And though we visit now to have unique experiences each time, unfortunately, I do not have any memories of taking either of my children to Disneyland as an infant, toddler, or preschooler - the iconic childhood stages where the innocence of Disney is at its best!

From a financial perspective, kids under the age of three do not have to pay park admission tickets, so many parents take advantage of this by visiting Disney before their child turns three.

On the other hand, many parents feel that they are spending so much money on a Disney vacation, they want to wait until their kids are a little bit older to ensure they remember the trip!

Both are valid viewpoints, and it will be up to your family to decide what works best for you.

The decision to take your kids to Disneyland for the first time is not to be taken lightly, but the minute you decide you are going to

Disneyland, I guarantee you will be filled with a joy and excitement you can't contain!

All the travel cliches are so real. Just like all the parenting cliches become real when you have kids. Just like all the sad and sappy songs make sense after you've had your heartbroken.

Travel is the best education. You learn things on a deeper level through experiences.

You will have stories of your adventures to tell because as you travel more, you will have more experiences. And you'll never forget those memories. The experiences and memories will help shape your children to see the world with new eyes.

The point of all this is to live in the now. Don't wait until someday. Live for today. Start planning today. And after each trip, you will start thinking about the next one. And the next one after that. Because travel becomes pretty addicting! Personally, I think it's a pretty good addiction to have and one I can deal with!

It doesn't have to be travel specifically, but more so experiences, rather than things. Travel just happens to be our life. And I'm here to help you travel more and have the courage to step out of your comfort zone, because everything about travel is uncomfortable and new. And that's part of the excitement with travel.

Whether it be a new destination, a new resort, or a new experience, there is always something new and unexpected that will take you out of your comfort zone. You learn to adapt - to explore, to learn, to try new things, to try new foods, new experiences - all of which will give you extraordinary memories and stories to tell. And that's what life is all about!

Think about all your travel dreams. What is it that you would like to see, experience, or visit? Why? Don't worry about the how. We can figure out how to make it happen.

Travelling with kids is definitely more challenging than travelling solo or with other adults. There are more details to be mindful of, and the challenges add a whole new layer to travel, which can be very intimidating and overwhelming at first. You can't be selfish with your itinerary anymore to save a few dollars (think red-eye flights, long layovers, or late nights). You also have to get comfortable with not having control over an already unfamiliar situation (which sometimes is very difficult for parents who you want to be in as much control as possible!). But as with everything else in life, the more you do it, the easier it becomes.

Disney is a safe place to start your travels, especially when your kids are young and you are ready to start taking on the added adventure of travelling as a family. It is the perfect place to introduce the trials and tribulations of travel and all the wonderful and educational experiences that come along with it. So much of Disneyland is inspired by Walt Disney's travels around the world that he wanted to bring it back with as much authenticity and accuracy as possible. He went to great lengths to ensure the experience was as real as he could recreate.

Walt Disney was a master storyteller and expanded his storytelling abilities through the experience of creating a theme park. And as a parent himself, Disney envisioned a family-friendly theme park that could be enjoyed by all, but most especially it was inspired by his two daughters.

And as parents, we are not that different. We all want to provide the best for our children. A trip to Disneyland will transform you and your family. Whether it be lessons learned through navigating the basic logistics of travel (packing, airport security, flight experiences, sleeping in unfamiliar accommodations) or the magical experience that a trip to Disneyland can bring, the memories your family will have are what makes it all worthwhile.

"Take vacations - memories more valuable than money. Can always make more money but cannot make more time.
Unknown

WELCOME TO THE DISNEYLAND RESORT

" To all those who come to this happy place: Welcome.
Disneyland is your land.
Here age relives fond memories of the past -
and here youth may savor the challenge and promise of the future. Disneyland
is dedicated to the ideals, the dreams, and the hard facts that have created
America - with the hope
that it will be a source of joy and
inspiration to all the world."
Walt Disney July 17, 1955

Disneyland is a beloved Southern California destination where generations of families have visited to make their Disney dreams come true, and it holds a special place in our hearts. It's a place where you come to find your favourite stories and characters come to life and experience the wonder and magic of how it all began.

Where else can you sail on the high seas with pirates, explore exotic jungles, meet fairy tale princes and princesses, step back into simpler times, and look ahead to the future all in one day? Disneyland Park is a magical kingdom where the imagination comes alive, families come together, magical memories are created, and Disney dreams come true. It is the cherished treasure of Southern California and the heart of Anaheim and Orange County where people from all over the world flock for an awe-inspiring experience.

The Disneyland Resort consists of two theme parks, **Disneyland Park** and **Disney California Adventure Park;** the **Downtown Disney District**, an area for exclusive dining, shopping, and entertainment experiences; and the hotels of the Disneyland Resort, **Disney's Paradise Pier Hotel**, **Disneyland Hotel,** and **Disney's Grand Californian Hotel & Spa**. Together, they make up the Disneyland Resort experience.

Disneyland is the original park that opened in July 1955. Disney California Adventure Park opened in 2001 as an homage to California, taking us back to a time where we can imagine the land that birthed all of Walt's dreams. Though it had somewhat of a slow start, California Adventure enjoyed a revitalization in 2012 when it went through a major transformation with the addition of Cars Land. This brought the park to a new level, providing the much-needed magic it was lacking.

Some background and history

Let's start with what is Disneyland. Simply put, it is unique in that there is nothing else quite like Disneyland.

It is a name that is recognizable around the world and is synonymous with a place that embodies happiness, joy, and wonder. It is the only Disney park that Walt Disney designed to completion, and the only one that he visited himself. Though he was originally a part of the Orlando expansion plans that would eventually become Walt Disney World, he sadly passed away in 1966, five years before its opening in 1971. As such, it was important for Roy Disney, his brother and business partner, to name the Orlando expansion project "Walt Disney

World" to ensure that Walt's legacy is carried on in Orlando. The vision of Walt Disney World was everything that Walt Disney wanted to create with Disneyland but wasn't possible in Anaheim.

But when we say "designed" it was that and so much more. Walt Disney designed every detail in Disneyland from the small to the grand to ensure a seamless and complete experience. His vision for Disneyland was to create a place of happiness and joy for families to come and escape, a place that is safe and clean, serviced by friendly and joyful staff, and a place to celebrate the joy of family and life in a timeless and trouble-free environment. Around each corner, you will see the Walt Disney touch, where attention to detail will fulfill a need or want you didn't know existed.

Even the layout of the park was carefully arranged with thought and attention. As soon as you walk under the bridge and into Disneyland, you are immediately transported back in time to small-town U.S.A. when times were simpler, life was slower, and everyone lived in small communities.

As you walk down **Main Street, U.S.A.**, you will see that the town is reminiscent of small towns in the U.S., where small mom-and-pop shops line the main street selling food, supplies, and fun. This is where people gather, and it leads you towards the Central Plaza, the central meeting point of Disneyland and home of Sleeping Beauty Castle.

From the **Central Plaza**, guests can choose from several different paths leading to a new land, each with its own unique experience but adding to the overall park experience. Embrace technology and the optimism of what the future can hold in **Tomorrowland**, or celebrate the imagination of childhood stories and dreams in **Fantasyland**. Preschoolers will feel like they have entered their favourite cartoon as Mickey Mouse and his friends welcome them home in **Mickey's Toontown**. Step into the Wild West in **Frontierland**, and enjoy exotic adventures in **Adventureland**. Connect with the beauty of nature and the animals of **Critter Country**, and then jam to the beat of **New Orleans Square**. Visit a galaxy far far away as you hyperspace into

Batuu, a remote outpost planet haven away from the prying eyes of the First Order in **Star Wars Galaxy's Edge**.

Disneyland is a timeless and trouble-free realm where you leave real life behind and surround yourself with happiness and joy. It inspires you to believe in the impossible. It is a place for guests to be completely free to play, explore, and enjoy the magic. The attractions were designed to tell stories rather than simply create thrills, and the immersive experience brings all the details to life in a magical world that exists outside of the real world.

Though Disneyland is the only park that Walt Disney saw to completion, his legacy and vision of what he wanted to create has transcended into a global imprint where millions of people continue to honour and carry out his dream. The global empire that Disney has become has included his significant influence from the beginning to bring joy and happiness to our daily lives, and the parks have become an idealistic "home" for many because the sights, sounds, and scents bring you back to your memories. Memories of happiness and joy, where our inner child can be fully expressed with glee and excitement in a place where we can be free to be ourselves.

BEFORE YOU GO

A little bit of planning can go a long way in helping you maximize your experience. For many, a Disneyland vacation is pretty high up on their family's bucket list. So you want to make sure that you review all the options available to ensure you are spending your time and money wisely for your family's specific needs. You will want to ensure you know your must-dos during your trip so you do not miss out on the most important experiences to you.

At the same time, don't try to do it all! It is a vacation after all, and you need to take the time to enjoy the experience as Walt intended. Every interaction, every attraction, and every show is about the complete and immersive experience. And there are so many things to do that it is impossible to do it all!

Planning a vacation to Disneyland is more than simply finding the right flights and choosing a hotel to stay. There are a lot of options to suit different families and their needs, budget, and preferences. Knowing all the options will help make your Disneyland vacation go a bit smoother and easier.

When is the best time to go?

This is one of the most commonly asked questions, and there really isn't a right answer. But generally, if you want to go when crowd levels are lower, then you will want to avoid peak times and holidays. Christmas is the busiest week at Disneyland, and parks commonly reach capacity levels during this week. Other extremely popular times include long weekends, spring break (which can include most of March and into April), Easter, American Thanksgiving, and the months of June, July, and August.

Best times to go:

- Mid-January through the first week in February End of April into mid-May
- September
- First week of November
- First two weeks of December

Why?

It will be less crowded and pricing for airfare and hotels will generally be lower during the above times.

However, during off-peak times, the weather may not be as ideal, refurbishments may be scheduled during that time, attractions may be closed down, and park hours may be shorter than usual. Also, some of the more popular entertainment options, including fireworks may not be scheduled. During the off season, fireworks are only scheduled on the weekends (Friday. Saturday and Sunday nights) so make sure you schedule a weekend day to visit Disneyland, if you are visiting in the off season.

September tends to be a really great time to visit as the weather is still pretty hot, and most families will be busy with the beginning of the school year so crowd levels will be lower, making it an ideal time to travel if you can.

October is another great time to visit, especially for Halloween fans! The Halloween season begins in mid-September through the month of October, however it impacts the park schedule as certain nights are closed early for the Halloween party.

The specially ticketed Halloween Party is a fun evening where guests are encouraged to dress up in costume, go trick or treating throughout the park, and enjoy specially themed food, entertainment and exclusive villainous character meet and greets while enjoying shorter lines for rides and attractions. On Halloween party ticket nights, guests will require a party ticket to enter the private party. Guests without Halloween party tickets will be asked to leave.

In previous years, Mickey's Not-So-Scary Halloween Party in Disneyland was the Halloween Party event. In 2019, Disney announced a new party taking place in Disney California Adventure. Oogie Boogie, from A Nightmare Before Christmas, summons all his villain friends for a frightfully fun night for the Oogie Boogie Bash.

Personally, I think the best time to travel is always in the first two weeks of December. Christmas decorations will be up, and you will be surrounded by Christmas spirit. The parks won't be as busy yet, so you can still enjoy all the Christmas festivities without it impacting your Christmas plans.

Most crowded times:

- Saturdays
- Sundays (during the summer and long weekends)
- Mid-February (Reading Week/Spring Break and long weekend)
- Most of March (Spring Break)
- Easter (including the week before and after Easter)
- Mid-June, July, and August (through Labor Day long weekend)
- American Thanksgiving in November
- Mid-December through first week of January

If you are somewhat restricted in your travel dates and you are travelling over a peak period, keep in mind that this is also the best time for everyone else to travel. Prepare for higher crowd levels and longer lines for everything from rides to restrooms.

The Christmas and New Year's time frame is the busiest time, and there may be days where the parks reach maximum capacity levels. When this happens, no admission is permitted into the parks so if you leave the parks on that day, you may not be able to enter again if it has reached capacity regardless of your tickets. So if you will be visiting the parks during these times, just don't leave or you risk not being able to get back in! If you want to be guaranteed entrance into the parks during very high capacity crowd periods, staying on-site at a Disney hotel will ensure you receive preferred admission to the parks with your theme park tickets.

Because Disneyland is a local park, weekends and holidays tend to be busier as there will be both out-of-town and local visitors to the parks.

Many local visitors are Annual Passholders, so it may be advantageous to check the Annual Passholder calendar for blockout dates. Blockout dates vary depending on the membership level of the Annual Passholder, so if you visit during a Passholder blockout period, you can be assured there will be less local visitors during that time.

When the parks get busy, they get busy. Just know that you will be waiting in line - lines to go through security, lines to enter the parks, line ups for food, restrooms, attractions, entertainment, character meet-and-greets, and purchasing souvenirs. All of them! You will want to scope out coveted viewing areas for fireworks and parades early as people will go early to secure preferred viewing areas.

However, just because the park gets busy and crowded doesn't necessarily mean you won't have a good time though so don't let the crowd calendars scare you from visiting! Disney has lots of great strategies and tools to help you make the most of your time despite the crowds and lines. You can optimize your time with options such as

Magic Morning (early morning park access one hour before opening to the general public); FASTPASS (complimentary); MaxPass (paid); and extra benefits for on-site Disney hotel guests.

FASTPASS allows guests to skip to the front of the lines for a specific time frame on a popular attraction and is included in all tickets. The addition of MaxPass allows you the convenience of selecting FASTPASS on your phone for some of the most popular attractions to maximize your time and minimize your overall wait times in the parks.

Weather in Anaheim

Overall, the weather in Anaheim is sunny and dry, making it an ideal place to visit all year round. Temperatures range from a low of 9°C (48°F) in the winter months to a high of 32°C (89°F) in the summer months.

During the winter months (November to April), temperatures are a bit cooler with possible rain. The average daytime temperature year-round is about 23°C (73°F). July, August, and September tend to be the hottest months, averaging 30°C (86°F). Days tend to be hot, but you may need jackets or light sweaters for the early mornings and evenings as it can get chilly.

How many days should you spend at the parks?

Disneyland sells 1-day to 5-day admission passes, so you can decide how many days you want to spend at Disneyland based on your overall vacation time.

Most common and recommended (3-day ticket)

For first-timers visiting Disneyland, you will want to visit the parks for a minimum of three days. This gives you one full day in each park and the third to do as you please. Although if you have the time to take advantage of the 5-day tickets, you will enjoy pretty much all of what

Disneyland offers at a pace that is leisurely and enjoyable with ample time to appreciate the experience.

Bare minimum (2-day ticket)

At a bare minimum though, two days to visit will allow you to enjoy each park. However, how much you see will also depend on crowd levels. If crowd levels are low, you will be able to see and do a lot in a short amount of time. Whereas on busier days, you may not get to experience as many attractions if there are long wait times. Utilizing the MaxPass service to select your FastPasses on your phone is highly recommended to conveniently maximize your time in the parks.

Ideal (4- to 5-day ticket)

Ideally, if you spend four or five days there, that will be plenty of time for you to enjoy all that the parks offer at a leisurely pace without feeling rushed or that you missed out on anything. Plus, it also includes plenty of time to experience your favourite attractions several times and to watch all the entertainment and nighttime spectacular experiences.

You won't feel rushed as you can tour the parks leisurely, with options to go early on one day, sleep in on others to stay later, catch a character meal or two, shop in the parks or at Downtown Disney, and enjoy some amazing dining experiences and some of the lesser-known experiences.

If you only have one day

If you only have one day to spend and opt for the base ticket with one park only, then spend it at Disneyland Park. It is the original park, and you might as well spend your day in the middle of the magic enjoying as much as you can. Arrive early, at least 60 minutes before park opening (or "rope drop"), to enter as soon as it opens.

If you have a Park Hopper pass for the day, you can go to both parks on the same day. Start in Disney's California Adventure Park first, and then end the day in Disneyland Park. You won't be able to see and experience it all, but you can fit in a few of the most popular attractions with a little bit of pre-planning and taking advantage of MaxPass!

For the first timers! If you are a first-time visitor and you only have one day, I would spend it all at Disneyland and wouldn't bother trying to hop between the two parks. There is so much magic to experience in Disneyland itself that you want to soak in as much as you can for the one day.

Head straight to the land you want to start exploring. While you may want to walk leisurely down Main Street, U.S.A, there will be plenty of time in the day to enjoy that.

If you have younger kids, you will want to head to Fantasyland or Mickey's Toontown.

If you have older kids - tweens or teens - you will probably want to start with either Tomorrowland or Adventureland, or Star Wars Galaxy's Edge for the Star Wars fans!

How many days you decide to spend at Disneyland will also be determined by your overall vacation goals. If you are planning on visiting other places in the Anaheim and Orange County area, you will need to factor in what other experiences you wish to include on the trip and plan accordingly.

What type of tickets should I choose?

In addition to the number of days for admission to the parks, you can choose from base tickets or Park Hopper tickets.

Base tickets

Base tickets provide admission to one park per day. So the park that you enter that day is the only park you can visit that day. It is unlimited admission for the day, so you can leave the park to take a break and return later in the day.

Park Hopper tickets

You can also upgrade the base tickets to Park Hopper tickets, which provide you with unlimited access to both parks on all days. You can go back and forth between both parks on the same day. The two parks are located close to each other, separated only by about a football-field size esplanade, so it is very convenient to visit both parks on the same day.

Important to note:

If you are not sure about Park Hopper tickets, you can always purchase base tickets and upgrade to Park Hopper tickets at any time before the tickets expire. Tickets expire 13 days from the date of first use. The price to upgrade to the Park Hopper is one flat price and will give you Park Hopper access on all days of your tickets. To maximize your Park Hopper access, upgrading earlier in your admission days will give you more flexibility on your park days.

Upgrading to Park Hopper tickets is also all-or-nothing. You either choose to purchase base tickets or Park Hopper for all days. You cannot mix base and Park Hopper tickets.

Multi-day tickets are valid for 13 days from the date of first use. One-day tickets are valid for that specific day and expire when the parks close. Tickets can be upgraded anytime as long as the tickets are valid and upgraded before the expiry date/time.

Children's tickets are available for kids ages 3-9. Adult tickets are for guests ages 10 and older. Children under the age of 3 are free. There is no cost for them to enter the parks, and there is no cost for them if you dine at any table service restaurant, including buffet restaurants.

One-day tickets

If you only have one day to spend at Disneyland, the ticket price for the 1-day ticket will vary based on the date of admission as tickets are priced by Peak, Regular, and Value season. Check the pricing calendar on the Disneyland website to determine which season your park day falls into.

If you have a 1-day ticket and decide you want to upgrade and add additional days, you can upgrade and pay only the difference between 1-day and 2-day tickets if you upgrade before the end of the day.

Magic Morning

If you purchase 3-day or more tickets in advance, you also receive one Magic Morning admission with your tickets. This allows you early morning access to Disneyland one hour earlier before it opens to the public so you can enter the parks and experience your favourite attractions with minimal wait times. Magic Morning is available on select days (Tuesday, Thursday, Saturday) when you can enter Disneyland one hour earlier before it opens to the general public.

Important to note:

Magic Morning is only available for Disneyland tickets (3-day or more) that are purchased in advance. Tickets purchased at the park gates do not include Magic Morning access and not all attractions are open during Magic Morning Hour.

FASTPASS (no longer available)

Disney's FASTPASS service is no longer available for all tickets and the program has been retired and replaced with the new Disney Genie, Disney Genie+ and Lightning Lane programs announced in August 2021 and debuting in December 2021. Select attractions provide the (formerly FASTPASS), but now Disney Genie+ and Lightning Lane service where you skip to the front of the line to access the attraction with minimal wait times.

DISNEY GENIE

Disney unveiled a brand new service, Disney Genie, to be your vacation assistant to help you plan and manage your Disney park days and maximize your time in the parks. Disney Genie is a complimentary service where you can obtain personalized recommendations to give you the best Disney day possible.

If you are familiar with the (formerly) FASTPASS program, you can obtain a FASTPASS for selection attractions and then you are given a specific one-hour time frame to return and head to the front of the line to experience the attraction. Once you have utilized that FASTPASS selection, you are free to obtain another FASTPASS for a different attraction. Now, the FASTPASS program has evolved into the Disney Genie program where you can utilize the Lightning Lane entrance to skip to the front of the line if you have .

The Lightning Lane access service is a great option to reduce waiting times for popular attractions so you can explore the rest of the park, grab a quick bite, and enjoy other attractions with shorter wait times.

There are two ways to access the Lightning Lane selections - either purchasing a single entry Lighting Lane access for select attractions, or through the addition of Disney Genie+ service, a paid service where you can access Lightning Lane selections one at a time, pre-selecting options one at a time from the convenience of your smartphone via Disney Genie, in the Disneyland app.

(Formerly) **MaxPass**

MaxPass was an optional ticket add-on to your tickets, regardless of the ticket type purchased that worked with the (formerly) FASTPASS program. If you were familiar with the MaxPass program, MaxPass gives you the ability to select your FASTPASS selections from the convenience of your smartphone with the Disneyland app so that you do not have to physically go to the kiosks to obtain a FASTPASS.

With the FASTPASS and MaxPass programs retired, the new additions of the complimentary Disney Genie program, Disney Genie+ program operates similar to the MaxPass program. With Disney Genie available through the Disneyland app, you can plan your day with real-time wait times for attractions to help you navigate through the day with personalized recommendations tailored to your preferences.

With Disney Genie+, the upgrade to the paid service allows you to pre-select attractions for select one hour windows where you can return to the attraction and access the Lightning Lanes to skip to the front of the lines for that attraction. Once you have used your Lightning Lane access, you can select your next Lightning Lane attraction access.

You can select a Lightning Lane for everyone in your party within the Disneyland app and easily cancel or change your selections from your smartphone. The app will also advise when you will be able to select the next Lightning Lane access. When it is time for you to experience the attraction, you simply head straight to designated Lightning Lane access.

Disney Genie+ also gives you unlimited access to and downloads for all photos and videos taken that day in the parks, including all character photos from meet-and-greets and Character Dining experiences, and all photos taken by Disney PhotoPass Photographers including Magic Shots and photos and videos from select attractions where available.

What's a Magic Shot? The Disney PhotoPass Photographer will ask you to pose a certain way or with a certain expression and it may not make sense to you at the time. But when you look at your photos later, there will be a "magical enhancement" with a Disney character that has been added to your photo!

Similar to the (formerly) MaxPass option, Disney Genie+ is an additional add-on per person per day and a limited number of MaxPass tickets are available each day, and your purchase is valid only for the day purchased.

Disney Genie+ is great to add on if the parks are busy, but it may not be necessary if crowds are low and wait times are minimal. You can decide if and when you would like to add it to your tickets as needed.

Insider tip! Because Disney Genie+ is optional and purchased on a per person basis, you can always just purchase Disney Genie+ for one person to receive unlimited downloads of the photos you take that day! This is what we do on a day where we want to focus on getting photos with characters more than riding attractions. It's perfect for your third or fourth days when you have likely experienced many of the attractions already and can focus on visiting with your favourite characters! And for the attractions with photos, you've likely already had them from previous days when you first enjoyed the attraction!

What else is in the area?

There are so many things to do in the area; all you need to decide is what else do you want to do! Just Disney or a SoCal vacation? Although some guests will visit Disneyland and only Disneyland, many guests will also take in other popular Southern California attractions during their stay. As part of your vacation planning, you may wish to review what other attractions you might want to visit during your trip.

Some of the more popular options for families include:

Universal Studios Hollywood

Universal Studios Hollywood is a theme park and film studio in the Los Angeles area (about one hour north of Anaheim) and a common day trip for Disneyland vacation guests. Day tours including transportation and tickets are available for guests who do not have access to a vehicle. The park is perfect for movie buffs as it is the only theme park with a working film studio and attractions centred around popular Universal Studios movies. It is also home of The Wizarding World of Harry Potter, an immersive magical world of wizards and a definite must-do for all Harry Potter fans!

Knott's Berry Farm

Commonly known as the "original theme park" thrill-seekers and local dwellers head to Knott's Berry Farm to enjoy over 40 wild rides for family fun for all ages. The amusement park is located in Buena Park, only 10 minutes from Disneyland.

LEGOLAND California

LEGO lovers will not want to miss visiting LEGOLAND in Carlsbad (about 100 km south of Anaheim), a theme park devoted to all things LEGO! Geared primarily towards kids under 12, the theme park includes LEGOLAND Park, SEA LIFE Aquarium, and CHIMA Water Park and two on-site LEGOLAND hotels to stay at with a choice of pirate, kingdom, adventure, and ninja LEGO themed rooms.

San Diego

Combine an Anaheim vacation with San Diego to take in popular family attractions in San Diego - namely, the San Diego Zoo, San Diego Zoo Safari Park, and SeaWorld San Diego.

Need a beach day?

With over 42 miles of coastline, there are plenty of beaches in the area for you to enjoy a relaxing beach day! Huntington Beach is the closest to Disneyland, but you can also enjoy the boardwalks of Santa Monica, Venice Beach, Laguna Beach, Balboa Island and Newport Beach as other nearby options.

There are also a lot of local favourite experiences in the Anaheim area. Working with a travel specialist who is familiar with Disneyland, Anaheim, and Southern California can really help you make the most of your trip to the area!

WHERE TO STAY

If your sole purpose of the trip is to visit Disneyland, then you may just want to stay in the Disneyland Resort area and not leave during your trip. Choose between either on-site options at one of the three Disney hotels or off-site in one of the Good Neighbor Hotels.

Staying at one of the Disneyland Resort hotels allows you to stay in the middle of the magic where the experience never ends! There are three Disneyland Resort hotels, and each has its own theme and unique selection of dining experiences and shopping opportunities fitting of its atmosphere and surroundings.

Disney's Grand Californian Hotel & Spa

The Grand Californian Hotel & Spa is the flagship hotel of the Disneyland Resort and offers premium accommodation, impeccable Disney service, and an ambiance of grand sophistication.

It is the closest hotel to the parks with its very own entrance into Disney California Adventure Park and it is located right in the middle of the Downtown Disney District.

The hotel has an upscale craftsman-style elegance and is an homage to California history and identity. Much of the architecture and design of the hotel pays tribute to California's rich and varied history. The rich brown wood beams provide nods to the Redwood trees of northern California creating a woodland theme throughout the hotel. In room details include counter top designs with pieces of green glass from wine bottles representing the award-winning wine valley regions of California. Copper detailing and California-inspired artwork of orange groves round out the intimate tributes to the home state. After completing an extensive refurbishment in 2017, the hotel is a truly luxurious retreat surrounded by the coziness of California.

Upscale dining experiences complement the extravagance of the Grand Californian Hotel experience.

Napa Rose Restaurant is an elegant and upscale family restaurant featuring California-inspired fare and award-winning wines. The fine-dining restaurant also features the signature princess experience, Disney Princess Breakfast Adventures, where guests enjoy a three-course breakfast meal with personal visits from Disney Princesses as well as fun activities, a personal Princess portrait moment, and a special keepsake memento of the experience. This special experience is available from Thursday through Sunday, and reservations are recommended.

Storytellers Cafe is where you will find Mickey Mouse for character breakfast or brunch dining adventures. Join Mickey and his gang on their global travel adventures as they visit each table for photos and autographs. Mickey's Tales of Adventure Breakfast Buffet and Mickey's Tales of Adventure Brunch Buffet include a large assortment of food options for breakfast or brunch, depending on the time of your dining reservation.

A dinner buffet is also available at the restaurant specializing in California-inspired dishes, but the characters do not appear during dinner.

Advance reservations are highly recommended and can be reserved 60 days in advance.

Disneyland Hotel

The Disneyland Hotel is a must for classic Disney fans who appreciate the history of Disneyland and Walt Disney himself. It is the original hotel built when Disneyland first opened in 1955 and embodies the complete spirit that is Disneyland, both the past and the present. It has been updated to include modern convenience and style with nods to the iconic past including classic Disneyland signage. The collage of Disney collectibles and milestones throughout the hotel commemorates the unique history of Disneyland.

Steps away from the Downtown Disney District, the hotel is a short walk through the Downtown Disney District to Disneyland Park and Disney California Adventure Park.

It is composed of three towers - the Adventure Tower, Fantasy Tower, and Frontier Tower - nods to the original lands of the park. The rooms are sophisticated yet whimsical, with details that embrace the classic years of Disneyland Park and its original innocence. Magical touches include light-up headboards featuring Sleeping Beauty Castle, fireworks, and a nighttime lullaby that is unique and endearing.

Signature Suites are perfect for giving an ultra spectacular themed touch for those who want an added experience to their hotel stay! Choose between themed pirate, princess, miner, or explorer suites or the ultimate VIP vacation experience in the grand Mickey Mouse Penthouse.

The on-site signature restaurant experiences include (formerly Steakhouse 55, which will re-open with a new restaurant option) and Goofy's Kitchen.

Steakhouse 55, (now since closed) was rich in Disney history, named for the year that Disneyland opened and provided a classic steakhouse experience within a glamorous Old Hollywood atmosphere. With a new restaurant to open in its place, there is no doubt the new theme will be just as elegant and classy, to fit with the Disneyland Hotel.

Goofy's Kitchen is a fun family buffet restaurant featuring Goofy and his friends where you can have a Character Dining experience at breakfast or dinner. It is the only restaurant that offers a Character Dining experience for dinner as all the other Character Dining experiences occur during breakfast only.

Expert tip! I recommend including a Character Dining meal at Goofy's Kitchen on your arrival day as it is the perfect intro to your Disney vacation. You get to meet all the main characters at dinner, and it gets everyone in the Disney mood! The characters are energetic and upbeat and interact in a way that will put a smile on your face and start your vacation with the right tone.

Disney's Paradise Pier Hotel

Celebrate and chill at Disney's Paradise Pier Hotel, the place where carefree California beach vibes provide a relaxing and laid-back stay. Step back in time to the early 1920s classic charm of California beachfront boardwalks with elegant, sea-inspired accommodations. The sunny and cheery ambiance adds to the old-fashioned feel of simpler times.

The rooftop pool terrace on the third floor is a favourite place to take in the California sun. It's also a great place to watch the fireworks show in Disneyland Park on select nights.

Recreation at all Disney hotels

Staying at any of the three Disney hotels permits you to enjoy the exclusive activities and facilities available only to guests of Disneyland Resort hotels such as the following:

A Magical Night at the Movies - Special screenings of popular Disney films are available on select nights.

Get Up & Go Power Walk - Guests are invited to join a very fast-paced two-mile power walk through Disney California Adventure Park at 6 a.m. for an exclusive fitness activity at the park.

Trivia Challenges - Put your Disney knowledge to the test as you hunt for answers to trivia questions at "the Happiest Place on Earth." Pick up a trivia question sheet at Guest Services and head to Disneyland Park to search for the answers. Once you have all the answers, head back to Guest Services to receive a special themed prize.

Art of Craft Tour at the Grand Californian Hotel - Open your eyes to all the magic embedded within the hotel and learn about the Arts and Crafts movement in California and how it influenced the architecture and design of the hotel. The tour provides a captivating behind-the-scenes glimpse into the many handcrafted artifacts found throughout the lobby and dining locations.

The Grand Quest at the Grand Californian Hotel - The Grand Quest is a scavenger hunt where guests can search for clues and uncover the secrets in a fun-filled, engaging, and interactive expedition. This quest is recommended for families with kids ages 3 to 12. Young adventurers will receive a special treat upon completion of the quest.

Benefits of staying on-site

Not only are you completely immersed in the experience, but staying on-site also provides a host of additional amenities to ensure you never leave the magic.

Extra Magic Hours

Receive early admission access one hour before the parks open to have the parks all to yourself for each day of your stay (though not all attractions are open during this hour). To maximize the early entry experience, it is recommended to arrive 1 hour and 15 minutes prior to park opening to provide sufficient time to get through security.

Proximity

All three Disney hotels are located within walking distance of the parks and Downtown Disney District including convenient access to the monorail station at Downtown Disney for transportation to and from Tomorrowland in Disneyland Park. Valid theme park admission is required, but it can be a handy option for taking a nice break from the park during the day to head back to your Disney hotel quickly and efficiently.

Preferred admission

You are guaranteed entrance into the parks, even if it has reached capacity for the day, especially during high peaks times (e.g. Christmas holidays).

Preferred access reservations

You receive preferred access reservations for popular Disneyland Resort restaurants or magical makeover experiences at the Bibbidi Bobbidi Boutique to make it easier for you to enjoy the Disneyland experience.

Access to the other Disney hotels

Enjoy resort-wide amenities at the other Disney hotels including the poolside cabanas and A Magical Night at the Movies experiences.

Cast Member assistance

Take advantage of round-the-clock assistance from Disney Cast Members to help make your stay enjoyable and effortless. Enjoy world-renowned Disney service through Cast Members' personalized assistance and their commitment to providing satisfaction.

In-room celebrations

In-room celebrations add a dash of pixie dust to commemorate your celebration or milestone - perfect for birthdays, anniversaries, personal achievements, romantic getaways, vacation welcomes, and character-themed surprises.

Charging privileges and package delivery

This convenient perk ensures you don't have to worry about carrying your souvenirs and purchases around the parks.

Character Dining

Disney Character Dining experiences are available at each of the Disney Resort hotels. Characters will stop by each table for photos and autographs and interact with the kids during your meal.

Disney Character Wake-Up Calls

Start each day of your stay with an early morning greeting from some of your favourite Disney characters. Contact Concierge Services to make the arrangements.

Complimentary luggage storage

Though check-in time is not until 3 p.m. on the day of your arrival, you can check in anytime and have your bags stored at Bell Services while you explore without having to wait for your room to become available. On your check-out day, you can store your bags without additional cost for the day until you are ready to leave Disneyland. This convenience allows you to enjoy all the other areas of Disneyland Resort without having to worry about luggage storage on your arrival and departure days.

Concierge level and suites

Suites are also available for those guests who want an elevated and exclusive Disney experience. Club Level rooms are available at each

Disney hotel - The Beachcomber Club at Disney's Paradise Pier Hotel, The E-Ticket Club at Disneyland Hotel, and The Verandah at the Grand Californian Hotel & Spa.

Fireworks viewing from Paradise Pier

Staying onsite at the Disney Hotels give you access to the facilities and amenities of the other Disney properties. The large pool patio area on the third floor of the Paradise Pier Hotel is open all Disney hotel guests and provide a fantastic view of the fireworks with the music piped in. Though you won't be able to see the projections on the castle, it can be a great way to experience the fireworks shows with accompanying music without the large crowds with a quick walk back to your room as soon as it's over.

Good Neighbor Hotels

As much as we all want to be immersed in the Disney experience, with only three on-site hotels to choose from, availability is limited, and they are all priced as Deluxe category hotels. Staying close to the magic doesn't have to cost an arm and a leg. There are plenty of Good Neighbor Hotels in the area with a variety of options suitable for every guest.

Good Neighbor Hotels are Disney-approved quality hotels that are close to the Disneyland Resort with moderate, superior, deluxe, and suite options for families of all sizes and budgets. As such, staying in a Good Neighbor hotel allows families to find something that fits their needs and budget, offering value without sacrificing quality and experience.

There are more than 40 Good Neighbor Hotels in the area, so there is a wide variety of choice, from big chain hotels to smaller boutique hotel options. Good Neighbor Hotels have been approved by Disney to ensure they provide quality amenities, service, price, and close proximity to Disneyland Park. The hotels are reviewed annually to maintain their Good Neighbor status. Most of the Good Neighbor Hotels are within walking distance or a short trolley ride away via the Anaheim Resort Transit (ART). Hotel stays can be combined with tickets to put together a convenient Disneyland Good Neighbor Vacation Package.

Advantages of staying at a Good Neighbor Hotel

Cost

Because of the wide variety of choice, there are hotel options for all budgets. For some guests, the hotel is simply a place to sleep and shower. Additional amenities are not required or desired as these guests will likely be spending most of their time in the parks and would prefer to spend their money in the parks over their accommodations.

Proximity

There are many affordable hotels located within walking distance to the parks, with some closer to the entrance than even the Disney hotels!

Hotels that are located a bit further away and not within ideal walking distance are serviced by the ART, a public transportation service that connects the hotels of Anaheim to Disneyland and several other popular Anaheim tourist attractions. The ART service is a great option for those who do not want to rent or drive a vehicle during their vacation. It also saves on parking fees as some hotels have nightly parking fees, especially the ones located closest to the parks.

Value

Many Good Neighbor Hotels also offer a complimentary shuttle service, free Wi-Fi, parking, and sometimes breakfast is included in the room rate.

Space

For larger families, there are hotels that can offer suites and spacious rooms to accommodate. It's just a matter of finding the right amenities to suit your needs and your budget.

ALL ABOUT DISNEYLAND PARK

8

DISNEYLAND PARK

Disneyland is the stage where Walt Disney could use his movie-making techniques and experiences to tell stories on a larger, three-dimensional stage. And he approached the park design to tell a story through the experiences of each land in a sequential format, just as you would if you were watching a movie or reading through chapters of a book.

Real-world travel experiences inspired many of the attraction designs and Walt Disney wanted to bring them to Disneyland, making it as authentic and true to life as possible. His attention to detail is what makes each experience so immersive, and each uniquely-themed land has its own story and special experiences that add to the layered experience of Disneyland.

Upon first arrival, you enter through the turnstiles and the large floral Mickey Mouse emblem welcomes you, signalling the fun you are about you have and setting the stage for your story ahead.

As soon as you walk underneath the bridge and through the tunnel, the world behind you ceases to exist and you gain entrance into a magical world full of adventure and fun. Regardless of how old you are, you cannot help but feel like you have entered another time and place, where imagination suspends belief.

"Here you leave today
and enter the world
of yesterday, tomorrow
and fantasy."

Entrance plaque on the bridge entering Disneyland Park

9

MAIN STREET, U.S.A.

DISNEYLAND PARK

Y ou first step back in time to the turn of the century, to a time where technology was starting to make a huge impact on our daily lives.

Electricity was becoming widely available, and the automobile was starting to become a more common form of transportation. The town plaza is where everyone gathered, where everyone knew each other, and the pace of life was much slower. Main Street, U.S.A. is modelled after the small town of Marceline, Missouri, where Walt Disney grew up, but the idea of the land was reminiscent of many of the small towns that made up the U.S. at the turn of the 20th century.

"Main Street, U.S.A. is America at the turn of the century - the crossroads of an era. The gas lamps and the electric lamp - the horse-drawn car and the auto car. Main Street is everyone's hometown - the heartline of America. Walt Disney, July 17, 1955, original Main Street, U.S.A. dedication

Stop by City Hall for any guest concerns, questions, or to pick up your complimentary celebration buttons. Take note of the Disneyland Fire Department, which you can enter to explore the fire truck inside.

There is an apartment above the Fire Hall where Walt Disney used to stay when working late at Disneyland so that he could oversee the park. It also had an adjacent private studio where Lillian, Walt's wife, could entertain guests for afternoon teas. The apartment is closed to the public, but there is a lamp in the window that is lit up in honour of Walt and his presence in the park. Make sure you look up and remember the man behind the magic.

Easy to miss as you first enter the park, is the Opera House on your right, which houses **The Disneyland Story presenting "Great Moments with Mr. Lincoln"**. This attraction provides a peek into Walt Disney's dream of creating the "Happiest Place on Earth" with a tribute to Abraham Lincoln, the 16th president of the United States, Walt Disney's favourite president and boyhood hero.

The streets of Main Street, U.S.A. are lined with small shops and restaurants, where you can meander from store to store chatting with people you meet along the way or stopping for sweet treats and refreshments. There is a comforting sense of childhood fun, idealistic and full of pure optimism, hope and adventure for what lies ahead.

One of the notable attractions in the area is the **Disneyland Railroad**, an authentic steam-powered train that has a stop in Main Street, U.S.A. Walt Disney was an avid train enthusiast whose vision of this theme park included having a train encircle the park. His childhood is filled with fond memories of trains as his father was a railroad mechanic and his uncle was a steam locomotive engineer.

The stop on Main Street, U.S.A. can connect you to other lands of the parks with stops in Tomorrowland, Mickey's Toontown, and New Orleans Square. But more than just a mode of transportation in the parks, it also provides a glimpse into history as you visit America's rugged landscapes through recreations of the Grand Canyon and

Primeval World - Land of the Dinosaurs. It's a great attraction to enjoy as a break from the busyness of the other rides.

The streets of Main Street, U.S.A. are also a great location to view the parades and the fireworks show at night with plenty of great viewing spots. For a front-row view though, you will need to get there early to scope out your spot.

Central Plaza (Hub)

As you head to the Central Plaza, the hub of the park, Sleeping Beauty Castle provides the focal point of the area and beckons you to come as you walk down Main Street.

In the center of the plaza, the iconic "Partners" statue of Walt Disney and Mickey Mouse is a popular photo location as it is directly in front of Sleeping Beauty Castle.

And then you come up to Sleeping Beauty Castle itself. And no words can describe the emotions you feel as you see the beauty of it up close. There is something about standing in front the castle, and all your senses are heightened to this one very moment that has made everything worthwhile.

Take as many photos as you can of your family and the castle! Disney PhotoPass Photographers will be on hand throughout Main Street, at the Parters statue and directly in front of the castle. Take the time to obtain all the photos because these are the ones that you and your kids will look back on years later and you are instantly transported back to this very moment in time. Serious, Sleeping Beauty Castle has that kind of magic!

From Central Plaza, you can head in different directions that will take you to distinctly different lands, each with its own unique experience.

In addition to Main Street, U.S.A., four other lands are directly accessible from the central hub (Tomorrowland, Fantasyland, Frontierland, and Adventureland), each providing a thoroughfare to the other four lands (Mickey's Toontown, New Orleans Square, Critter Country, and Star Wars: Galaxy's Edge).

Sleeping Beauty Castle anchors guests as they navigate through the lands and provides you with the sense of familiarity and comfort as you walk through the park. You can always see Sleeping Beauty Castle and head to the hub area to regroup, never feeling like you will get lost in the park.

10

TOMORROWLAND
DISNEYLAND PARK

B last off into space and head to the land of tomorrow, where the future is bright and optimistic and full of hope and adventure. With a bit of practicality and a lot of imagination, Tomorrowland provides a land of forward-thinking and intellectual ideals in a hopeful innocent view of the future.

"A vista into a world of wondrous ideas, signifying man's achievements ... a step into the future, with predictions of constructed things to come. Tomorrow offers new frontiers in science, adventure and ideals: the Atomic Age ... the challenge of outer space and the hope for a peaceful and unified world."
Walt Disney, July 17, 1955, original Tomorrowland dedication

Notable attractions to experience in this popular land include:

Space Mountain

Always a favourite for thrill-seekers, this roller coaster ride skyrockets you into space!

Passengers must be free of back problems, heart conditions, motion sickness, and other physical limitations. It is not advisable for pregnant women to go on this ride. There is a minimum height requirement of 40 in. (102 cm) to ride. Children under 7 must ride with an adult.

Seasonal overlays are sometimes available. Ghost Galaxy is an overlay during the Halloween season and Hyperspace Mountain puts you in the middle of a Star Wars-themed adventure.

Star Tours - The Adventures Continue

Join the adventure on this 3D motion simulated space journey. There are more than 50 different adventures loaded into the attraction, so you can ride it multiple times and never have the same experience.

Passengers must be free of back problems, heart conditions, motion sickness, and other physical limitations. It's not advisable for pregnant women to go on this ride. There is a minimum height requirement of 40 in. (102 cm) to ride.

Buzz Lightyear Astro Blasters

Guests can help Buzz Lightyear fight against the Evil Emperor Zurg. This is a fun ride for all ages, and kids love the chance to shoot their blasters at the bad guys and see their score at the end.

Insider tip! The diamond and triangle shaped targets are worth the most points! Clues about scoring points can be found throughout the queue leading up to the attraction.

Autopia

Kids who love to pretend to drive will not want to miss Autopia, a miniature roadway where guests can drive in a car with a real working gas pedal and steering wheel.

This ride is specially designed for kids. Guests who are at least 54 in. (137 cm) tall can drive on their own, and kids who are at least 32 in. (81 cm) can drive and steer as long as there is someone at least 54 in.(137 cm) tall with them. Each car can seat 2 adults or 3 kids. Kids under the age of 7 must be accompanied by someone at least 14 years of age. Passengers must be free of back problems, heart conditions, motion sickness, and other physical limitations. It's not advisable for pregnant women to go on this ride.

Disneyland Monorail

The Disneyland Monorail station is located in Tomorrowland and offers quick transportation from the park to the Downtown Disney District. It's close to the Disney on-site hotels so it's very convenient if you are staying at any of their properties. The station is located at the Downtown Disney District station, offering great views of the park as you head straight to Tomorrowland in Disneyland Park, skipping the Main Entrance. (Valid theme park admission is required to board the Disneyland Monorail from the Downtown Disney District station.)

Park guests can take a ride in the Disneyland Monorail and either get off at the Downtown Disney District station for a break from the park, or ride a roundtrip journey from Tomorrowland.

Insider tip! If available, ask to sit in the front for fantastic views of your journey! Only four guests are permitted at a time to ride in the front of the Monorail so space is not always available but it's worth a shot.

The Disneyland Monorail was the first of its kind when it first opened in 1959, and the current monorail combines new technology with zero-emission exhaust or pollutants. The pool slides at the Disneyland Hotel pay homage to the Disneyland Monorail's retro-futuristic design.

11

FANTASYLAND
DISNEYLAND PARK

In Fantasyland "The Happiest Kingdom of them All", the wonder and magic of Disney fairy tales come to life, and guests are transported to a timeless realm of childhood imagination.

"Here is the world of imagination, hopes and dreams. In this timeless land of enchantment, the age of chivalry, magic and make believe are reborn and fairy tales come true. Fantasyland is dedicated to the young and the young-at-heart - to those who believe that when you wish upon a star, your dreams do come true."
Walt Disney, July 17, 1955, original Fantasyland dedication

Sleeping Beauty Castle provides a gateway to the "Happiest Kingdom of Them All." As you walk through the castle, you can climb up the stairs to step into the story of Princess Aurora, told through dioramas. The three-dimensional displays, sounds, and special effects bring the story of Sleeping Beauty to life, complete with the evil Maleficent transforming into a fire-breathing dragon!

"Once upon a time".... the classic beginning of all fairy tales begins here at Fantasy Faire. Meet all your favourite princesses at Royal Hall and

Tinker Bell and her fairy friends at Pixie Hollow. Watch your favourite Disney stories come to life on stage at the Royal Theatre.

Fantasyland has 13 attractions in the area, with many of them that are unique to Disneyland in Anaheim, not found in any other Disney parks in the world and also has the largest number of attractions for young kids.

Notable attractions in Fantasyland include the following:

Peter Pan's Flight

One of the most classic and popular rides. Prepare for long wait times as FASTPASS is not available for this attraction. Head here either first thing in the morning or later on in the day for shorter wait times.

Matterhorn Bobsleds

One of the more thrilling rides at Disneyland and one of the four "mountains" that can be conquered (in addition to Space, Splash, and Big Thunder Mountains). Inspired by the Swiss Alps, the jolting ride takes you up into the mountain with twists and turns, and you come in contact with and escape from the Abominable Snowman.

There is a minimum height requirement of 42 in. (107 cm). The ride is very fast and bumpy. Passengers must be free of back problems, heart conditions, motion sickness, and other physical limitations. It's not advisable for pregnant women to go on this ride.

Must do! This attraction is unique to Disneyland in Anaheim as it is not in any of the other Disney parks around the world. When it first debuted in 1959, it was the first tubular steel roller coaster in the world and set the stage for roller coaster designs going forward.

Insider tip! For a shorter wait time, and/or for spectacular views, ride the attraction during the fireworks or late at night.

"it's a small world"

This attraction features a whimsical boat ride around the world with cheerful dolls in their culturally native attire singing a unified song in their native languages. Almost 300 Audio-Animatronic dolls, featuring over 100 regions of the world, are included in the attraction heralding world peace for all.

Insider tip! The area in front of the attraction is also one of the places in the park that provides a great viewing location for parades and fireworks.

Bibbidi Bobbidi Boutique

Every little princess dreams of getting a most magical makeover, and the Fairy Godmother can make it all come true! Choose from a simple hair and makeup package to the full makeover experience with princess gown and all. Your little ones will be pampered until they become a true Disney princess! The Bibbidi Bobbidi Boutique princess makeover experience is available for kids ages 3 -12 and is a highly recommended must-do for little girls and princess lovers!

The boys don't have to miss out on the experience either as they have knights packages to turn them into the mighty heroes they are. They are not quite as elaborate as the princess experience but provide just enough of an experience for boys to not feel left out.

Although I waited until my kids were a bit older to take them to Disneyland, I do wish that I had taken my little girl to Disneyland when she was much younger to be able to enjoy the Bibbidi Bobbidi Boutique experience; both for her enjoyment and for me to experience it as a parent. When she was younger, she was just like all the little girls who wanted to be a princess! By the time we started experiencing Disney as a family, she had outgrown the princesses and was not interested in the Bibbidi Bobbidi Boutique or the princess makeover experience.

So if you have a little princess in your family, make sure you do the Bibbidi Bobbidi Boutique before they outgrow the princess stage as it is such a magical experience for the girls and their parents to enjoy!

Reservations can be made 60 days in advance and are highly recommended. Guests staying on-site at a Disney hotel will receive preferred reservation times and opportunities. A credit card is required at the time of reservation but will not be charged until the time of appointment. Cancellations without penalty can be made up to 24 hours before your appointment. There is a $10 cancellation fee for no shows or any cancellations within 24 hours of your appointment time.

Insider tip! Ideal appointment times are mid to late morning so that you have some time to enjoy the park before making your way to the salon, with lots of time remaining in the day for plenty of photo opportunities!

Insider tip! Save money by bringing your own princess dresses from home and make sure you purchase dressed at least half a size larger for maximum comfort in the parks.

12

FRONTIERLAND

DISNEYLAND PARK

*"Here we experience the story of our country's past - the colorful drama of
Frontier America in the exciting days of the covered wagon and the stage
coach ... the
advent of the railroad ... and the romantic riverboat. Frontierland is a tribute
to the faith, courage and ingenuity of the pioneers who blazed the trails across
America."*
Walt Disney, July 17, 1955, original Frontierland dedication

Head back to America's Old West of the 19th century where cowboys and pioneers were exploring the land and in search of gold. Explore the rugged landscapes of the mountains and dense forests along the banks of America in the era of riverboats, railroads, wagons, and stagecoaches.

The most notable attraction in the land is **Big Thunder Mountain**, a fun roller coaster that takes you through a wild ride in the wilderness. The attraction is an original Disney creation, based on an old Indian legend about a sacred mountain in Wyoming. If anyone tried to excavate its gold, it would roar and thunder to scare people away. And legend has it that eerie events started to happen after gold was discovered in the 1850s. Trains would mysteriously take off and race through tunnels.... by themselves.

It is a fairly tame roller coaster ride, though there is a minimum height requirement of 40 in. (102 cm). Kids under the age of 7 must be accompanied by a guest age 14 or older.

Passengers must be free of back problems, heart conditions, motion sickness, and other physical limitations. It's not advisable for pregnant women to go on this ride.

The **Rivers of America** in Frontierland is dedicated to exploring the four iconic rivers of the Midwest - the Mississippi, the Columbia, the Missouri and the Rio Grande encircling the **Pirates Lair on Tom Sawyer Island**. This secret island hideaway was inspired by the stories of Mark Twain (another of Walt Disney's boyhood heroes) and the carefree adventures of Tom Sawyer and Huckleberry Finn.

Take a relaxing 14 minute boat ride to explore the Rivers of America onboard one of two ships, the **Mark Twain Riverboat** (an authentic steam powered vessel) or the **Sailing Ship Columbia** (a full scale replica of the 18th century Columba Rediviva, the first American ship to circumnavigate the globe and namesake of Oregon's Columbia River) or paddle along the river in the free floating canoes of **Davy Crockett's Explorer Canoes** (which can be accessed from Critter County)

Please note: some attractions in the Rivers of America area are closed in the evenings for the popular nighttime spectacular "Fantasmic!", as it takes place on the Rivers of America.

13

ADVENTURELAND
DISNEYLAND PARK

"Here is adventure. Here is romance. Here is mystery.
Tropical rivers - silently flowing into the unknown.
The unbelievable splendor of exotic flowers ... the eerie sound of the jungle ...
with eyes that are always watching.
This is Adventureland."
Walt Disney, July 17, 1955, original Adventureland dedication

Adventure to the faraway and mysterious jungles of Asia, Africa, South America, and the South Pacific during a time when explorers ventured into unknown realms full of natural wonder. After exploring Africa and Asia for his nature documentaries, Walt Disney wanted to recreate the intrigue of the exotic and remote tropical jungles and bring the experience to Disneyland where visitors may not otherwise have the opportunity to discover these parts of the world.

Notable attractions to experience in this area include:

Jungle Cruise

Cruise through the exotic rivers of the Amazon in South America, the Nile in Africa, and the Irrawaddy and Mekong rivers of Asia in a riverboat with a skipper. Cheesy jokes, puns, and the deadpan expressions of the skipper are the highlight of the Jungle Cruise experience, so it is never the same if you repeat the ride with a different skipper.

Did you know? Walt Disney originally wanted to have real animals for the attraction but when he discovered that real animals might not always be visible or entertaining for the storyline, he commissioned the animatronic animals so that they would always be relevant to the story.

Also, over the holiday season, the Jungle Cruise becomes the "**Jingle Cruise**" with a holiday overlay and new storyline to enjoy.

Indiana Jones Adventure

Join an expedition through the ancient Temple of the Forbidden Eye, built to honour the powerful deity of Mara. Legend claims that Mara can grant one of three gifts: unlimited wealth, eternal youth, or future knowledge. However, those who gaze directly into the eyes of Mara will succumb to a terrible fate. Creative imagineering through the ride allows for slightly different outcomes, so you can ride the attraction several times without it being the same experience.

There is a minimum height requirement of 46 in. (117 cm) to ride, and it can get dark and scary so it may not be suitable for young kids. Kids under the age of 7 must be accompanied by a person age 14 or older. Passengers must be free of back problems, heart conditions, motion sickness, and other physical limitations. It's not advisable for pregnant women to go on this ride.

Walt Disney's Enchanted Tiki Room

Tucked away in Adventureland and easy to overlook is Walt Disney's Enchanted Tiki Room, the first of the park's Audio-Animatronics attractions, featuring over 225 singing parrots in a pseudo-Polynesian show. It's a delightfully entertaining show, offering a cool indoor break when needed.

Enjoy the famous DOLE Whip soft-serve dessert sold right outside the entrance!

Tarzan's Treehouse

Explore the treehouse home of Tarzan in the jungle as you climb up an 80-foot tall tree, cross the suspension bridge for incredible views and wild explorations from above.

Perfect for some down time or a place for kids to burn off extra energy, the treehouse is an exploration in adventure with hands-on interactive experiences.

14

MICKEY'S TOONTOWN
DISNEYLAND PARK

Mickey's Toontown is a whimsical recreation of a cartoon town, inspired by the movie *Who Framed Roger Rabbit*, where Mickey Mouse and his friends live and the cartoon world comes alive. Animation is brought to life with colourful and wacky designs. The bustle of downtown combined with the charm of the residential houses of the characters make the whole town fun and exciting for young kids to explore for hours. Everything in Toontown is meant to be interactive, so kids are encouraged to touch and play as much as they want to.

According to the legend, Toontown has always existed but was kept secret from the public. It was the place where Mickey Mouse lived after he retired from the movies and wanted to get away from the glare of Hollywood. But when Walt Disney was looking for a location to build Disneyland, it was Mickey Mouse who suggested he build it next to Toontown. It wasn't until 1993 that Mickey and his friends decided to open up their secret town to non-toon guests for everyone to explore.

. . .

Toontown operates on its own opening hours, so guests should be aware of this before entering. It opens one hour after the park opens, and it closes one hour before the park closes on evenings when there is a fireworks show, due to the proximity of the fireworks launch.

Roger Rabbit's Car Toon Spin

The main attraction in Toontown is a chaotic spinning and dizzying car chase with Roger Rabbit and Benny the Cab in a mission to save Jessica Rabbit. It is a fun and wacky ride, but there are times where it may be too dark or rough for young kids. FASTPASS is available for this attraction and is highly recommended.

Toontown is a popular place for the younger kids and can get very busy, especially in the afternoon. Bring you cameras and autograph books as you can meet Mickey Mouse, Minnie Mouse and Goofy in person at their respective homes.

Mickey & Minnie's Runaway Railway

Announced by Disney at the D23 Expo in Anaheim on August 19, 2019, Mickey and Minnie will be receiving their very first ride-through attraction at Disneyland Park.

Guests will be put inside the middle of a wacky cartoon short and experience the unpredictable adventures with Mickey, Minnie and Goofy in the cartoon world.

15

NEW ORLEANS SQUARE

DISNEYLAND PARK

E scape to the sights and sounds of the South when in New Orleans Square, the last major project that Walt Disney was involved in before he passed away in 1966. The elegance of the area is carefully recreated with intricate architecture, embedding the culture and music of the French Quarter. It is a celebration of the city, its energy, music, and food that he loved and even incorporated relics that he brought back from his visits to New Orleans.

The attractions in the area, Pirates of the Caribbean and Haunted Mansion, are the last attractions that Walt Disney had creative input and influence in their design.

Pirates of the Caribbean

A fun swashbuckling boat ride that inspired a multi-billion-dollar movie franchise, the Pirates of the Caribbean attraction takes you through a pirate's life with a story full of scallywags and pillaged plunder. The character of Captain Jack Sparrow and his schemes to steal guarded treasures are the highlights of the story told through intricate details, special effects, and memorable characters. It's always a fan favourite and boasts long wait times during busy seasons.

A unique dining experience is inside the attraction at the Blue Bayou Restaurant, featuring Cajun and Creole specialties while enjoying the ambiance of the attraction.

Located above the Pirates of the Caribbean attraction is the Disneyland Dream Suite, a private 2,200 square foot apartment that Walt Disney had built for himself but passed away before it was fully completed.

Haunted Mansion

The Haunted Mansion is a home for ghosts who became homeless and were left wandering the streets when their previous mansions were torn down. These ghosts wander and tell their stories through "spirited entertainment". The intention of the attraction was not to make a frightening ride, but more of an eerie but frightfully amusing attraction that transitions from dark and spooky to entertaining with loads of special effects and intricate details.

During the holiday season, the attraction becomes Haunted Mansion Holiday, receiving a seasonal overlay with Jack Skellington and the characters from "The Nightmare Before Christmas". The seasonal overlay starts during the Halloween season and runs through the holidays season complete with jack-o-lanterns and holiday wreaths to complement the attraction.

Must try! Mickey-shaped beignets are a must-do Disney treat and can be found at the Mint Julep Bar or Cafe Orleans in New Orleans Square.

Did you know? Also located in New Orleans Square is Club 33, an exclusive, private membership-only lounge.

16

CRITTER COUNTRY

DISNEYLAND PARK

Relax with nature in the lush and shady forests of Critter Country where playful animals find their joy. Woodland creatures from the briar and Winnie the Pooh and friends inhabit the land. Tucked near the far end of the park, it provides a quiet and relaxing break from the hustle and bustle of the other areas of the park.

Splash Mountain

One of the most popular attractions in Disneyland is Splash Mountain. Originally based on the animated sequences in Walt Disney's 1946 film *Song of the South*, the attraction is being re-imagined to a new a new theme featuring Princess Tiana and her loyal sidekick Louis, from The Princess and the Frog. The ride takes you on a musical adventure as Princess Tiana and Louis prepare for their grand musical performance at Mardi Gras, set in the backdrop of New Orleans and the Louisiana bayou. As you reach the end, you "drop" 50 feet down in a sharp angle for a fast and thrilling ride, and you will get wet!

Kids must be a minimum of 40 in. (102 cm) tall to ride. And kids under the age of 7 must be accompanied by a guest age 14 or older.

FASTPASS is available for this attraction but lines can be long, especially in the afternoons, during the hottest times of the day and during peak times.

Insider tip! Try to sit near the back if you don't want to get too wet. If your party does not need to sit together, utilizing the single rider line can mean much shorter wait times.

The Many Adventures of Winnie the Pooh

Everyone's favourite honey-loving cub has his own attraction. You board beehives to get a wild and whimsical tour of the Hundred-Acre Wood. This ride is a little wacky and adventurous with Pooh Bear and his friends making it a fun and cute attraction for all ages.

Davy Crockett's Explorer Canoes

Explore the Rivers of America and all around Pirates Lair on Tom Sawyer Island in hand-paddled canoes, just as the legendary 19th century explorer travelled. The canoes are free-floating vessels without any motor or track to follow. They hold a maximum 20 passengers who paddle to experience travel as early Native Americans and European explorers would have travelled.

Insider secret! You don't really have to paddle! Most of it is more for fun than anything else as the river guides are capable of navigating it for your enjoyment.

Please note: The canoes operate seasonally, and may close due to inclement weather, and is only open during certain times of the day. If this is something you wish to experience, it is recommended to head here early in the day.

17

STAR WARS: GALAXY'S EDGE

DISNEYLAND PARK

The newest land to open in Disneyland is Star Wars: Galaxy's Edge, which opened on May 31, 2019 - the largest expansion plan in Disney history and based on the Star Wars franchise. There are three entrances to Star Wars: Galaxy's Edge - from Fantasyland, Frontierland and Critter Country.

As a completely original storyline, Galaxy's Edge is a part of the Star Wars overall story but unique at the same time. The land is Batuu, a gateway planet located on the outer rim of the Galaxy, and the village is Black Spire Outpost. The setting of the land takes place within the sequel trilogy, after the events of *Star Wars: The Last Jedi* but before *Star Wars: Rise of Skywalker*. Though it exists in the Star Wars universe, all the stories and experiences are original, so guests can be immersed in the universe and create their own stories and experiences.

Millennium Falcon: Smugglers Run

This is your chance to fly the Millennium Falcon on a thrilling ride through hyperspace! It's the only ship to make the Kessel Run in less than twelve parsecs! The interactive ride puts you in one of three available positions in the cockpit, (pilot, gunner, or engineer), each with a crucial role in determining the success of the mission. Travellers pilot the Millennium Falcon in an adventure to collect precious, not-very-legal cargo and win points for the Resistance. Each person works as a part of a team for the mission, and the more successful the ride, the more credits you can earn and the longer the ride becomes.

There is a minimum height requirement of 38 in. (or 97 cm) to ride.

Rise of the Resistance

The flagship attraction of the land, Rise of the Resistance is now open and it is one of the most advanced and immersive experiences of any Disney attraction. Combining fantasy and reality, riders can become the lead of their very own Star Wars film and experience the greatest challenge of the First Order.

Guests are recruited to join Rey and General Organa in a secret location. Along the way, they are captured by a First Order Destroyer. With the help of some heroes of the Resistance, they will break out and escape the Star Destroyer, as a part of an epic battle between the First Order and the Resistance.

This state-of-the-art experience combines four attractions-in-one, a 28 minute long experience from start to finish, featuring 18 show areas and 5 ride systems through the biggest attraction show building ever created. It includes over 305 animatronic figures including Stormtroopers and droids.

A virtual queue boarding pass system has been introduced and guests must obtain a Boarding Pass from the Disneyland app in order to get into the queue to enjoy the ride. Boarding Passes can be obtained each day at 7:00 a.m and 12:00 p.m. each day.

Oga's Cantina

Though it's not necessarily an "attraction" or a ride, Oga's Cantina is an experience that is highly recommended to enjoy. Oga's Cantina is the watering hole on the edge of the galaxy where smugglers, traders, and travellers come together after long travel days or to discuss "business" while enjoying the music of droid DJ R-3X, a former StarSpeeder 3000 pilot from Star Tours - The Adventures Continue in Tomorrowland. Out of this world beverages and concoctions are available, including alcoholic beverages. (Oga's Cantina is the first and only place within Disneyland Park to offer alcohol. Beverages can only be consumed in the restaurant and cannot be taken out of the building.)

Space is very limited, so reservations are highly recommended. Reservations can be made directly in the Disneyland app on your smartphone. Seats are also very limited, so most of the interior is standing room only. To ensure a smooth and enjoyable experience for guests, there may be a time limit on your visit.

Savi's Workshop

Star Wars fans will also have the opportunity to build their very own customized lightsaber in a covert location away from the watchful eyes of the First Order.

Bring the light sabre to life through the power of cyber crystals and select from one of four themes to design your lightsaber:

- **Peace and Justice** - salvaged scraps from fallen Jedi temples and crashed starships in Republic-era designs that honour the galaxy's former guardians.
- **Power and Control** - originally forged by warriors of the dark side, the objects are rumoured to be from the Sith homeworld and abandoned temples.
- **Elemental Nature** - born from the Force, these components

contain energy from all living things, including Brylark trees, Cartusian whale bones and Rancor teeth.

- **Protection and Defence** - reconnect users to the ancient wellspring of the Force

The experience is limited to one lightsaber per person per experience with two guests permitted to join the builder. Reservations are highly recommended and can be made directly in the Disneyland app on your smartphone.

Droid Depot

To have a trusty assistant and sidekick in the galaxy, you can build your very own droid at the Droid Depot. Choose which unit you want to build - either the BB-series or the R-series - and you will be provided with a blueprint and the proper parts to assemble the droid before activating it and watching it come to life!

ALL ABOUT DISNEY CALIFORNIA ADVENTURE

DISNEY CALIFORNIA ADVENTURE

Disney California Adventure Park pays tribute to the Golden State, celebrating the history and culture of California, but with a Disney focus. There are seven unique lands, each set in a historic time period of California to highlight the appeal to those looking for adventure.

Buena Vista Street represents Los Angeles as it may have looked when Walt Disney arrived in 1920. **Hollywood Land** celebrates the golden age of movies and glamour during its heyday. **Pacific Wharf** takes you to the iconic California coast of San Francisco and Monterey, and **Pixar Pier** showcases the seaside amusement parks with a Pixar twist with **Paradise Gardens Park** complementing the pier area. **Cars Land** is a recreation of the town of Radiator Springs from the movie *Cars*. **Grizzly Peak** celebrates the natural beauty and rugged mountain landscapes.

Avengers Campus, a new Marvel-themed superhero land (formerly A Bug's Life) is where all your favourite Marvel superheroes will unite to protect the universe (opened June 2021).

"To all who believe in the power of dreams, welcome. Disney's California

Adventure opens its golden gates to you. Here we pay tribute to the dreamers of the past: the native people, explorers, immigrants, aviators, entrepreneurs and entertainers who built the Golden State. And we salute a new generation of dreamers who are creating the wonders of tomorrow, from the silver screen to the computer screen, from the fertile farmlands to the far reaches of space. Disney's California Adventure celebrates the richness and the diversity of California ... its land, its people, its spirit and, above all, the dreams that it continues to inspire.
Michael Eisner, February 8, 2001, original Disney's California Adventure dedication

Disney California Adventure theme park opened in 2001 with its original intention to showcase California, the home state of Disneyland. But as a result of the challenges presented by international Disney plans (*think Euro Disney*) during the 1990s, the initial Disneyland expansion plans were significantly scaled down, with many of the original ideas discarded in favour of a substantially trimmed budget.

As a result, the initial opening of Disney's California Adventure suffered from mediocre reviews, disappointing attendance, and lacklustre response. The park was viewed by many as tacky and corny, and it failed to live up to Disney standards for quality, theming, or popularity. Critics were quick to note the lack of attractions for young children, the park's uninspiring theme, and the lack of a "Disney" ambiance with no shows or entertainment to keep guests in the park into the evening.

The park continued to evolve and add attractions and entertainment to improve its appeal, but it wasn't until Disney committed to a billion dollar large scale expansion plan for Disney's California Adventure that things began to improve. The vision included a complete overhaul to transform the park into an experience equal to its sister park, Disneyland. The original theme celebrating California was scrapped, and imagineers went to work to re-theme the park.

On June 15, 2012, Disney's California Adventure was renamed to Disney California Adventure Park (dropping the possessive form of Disney) and it was opened as a new park, taking guests back in time to the adventures of Walt Disney when he first arrived in California. The entrance and existing lands were transformed into what is now known as Buena Vista Street and Hollywood Land, and a completely new immersive park experience called Cars Land was introduced.

The park is still themed to its home state of California, celebrating its history and culture through the stories of Disney, Pixar, and Marvel. The revitalization of the park turned it from a modern spoof of California into a romanticized idealized version of the state, exploring specific time periods and historic settings.

The park was rededicated to showcase its new beginnings and a new era for the Disneyland Resort.

"To all who come to this place of dreams, welcome. Disney California Adventure celebrates the spirit of optimism and the promise of endless opportunities, ignited by the imagination of daring dreamers such as Walt Disney and those like him who forever changed - and were forever changed by it - The Golden State. This unique place embraces the richness and diversity of California ... Its land, its people, its stories and, above all, the dreamers it continues to inspire."
Robert Iger, June 15, 2012, rededication of Disney California Adventure

The entrance to Disney California Adventure is a replica of the entrance to the old Pan-Pacific Auditorium in Los Angeles, which is the same design for the entrance to Disney's Hollywood Studios at Walt Disney World in Orlando, Florida. As you enter the park, you will step back in time to 1920s Los Angeles as it may have looked when Walt Disney first arrived to California.

Walk the streets as Walt would have. Right at the entrance of Buena Vista Street, stop to pay attention to the flagpole, where you will see the rededication plaque and beside it a time capsule buried for 25 years, to be opened on June 15, 2037.

May the hopes and dreams represented by the collection contained within the time capsule beneath this marker inspire a future generation of dreamers when it is unsealed a quarter of a century from now, on June 15, 2037.

19

BUENA VISTA STREET

DISNEY CALIFORNIA ADVENTURE

Buena Vista Street provides an experience akin to Main Street, U.S.A. in Disneyland, representing the streets of Los Angeles during the time when Walt Disney first arrived in 1923. Young and full of dreams and ideas, Walt arrived with grand visions to make his mark in animation history. The name Buena Vista Street came from the street where Walt Disney Studios is located in Burbank, California, and provides an immersive recreation of early 1920s Los Angeles, giving guests the impression of walking in Walt's footsteps.

The decor and facades of the buildings are an idyllic representation of Los Angeles, invoking a sense of grand dreams, energy, and vigour. All of the architecture along Buena Vista Street represents key moments, events, or backstories of the Walt Disney Company and Walt Disney's personal history.

Oswald's is one of the first stores you encounter, inspired by Oswald the Lucky Rabbit, one of Walt Disney's first successful cartoon characters. Unfortunately, he lost the property rights to the character in a contract dispute, which inspired him to create Mickey Mouse, and he vowed to retain complete control over every intellectual property from that time on.

As you walk down Buena Vista Street, the business names and addresses have historic significance or pay tribute to Disney history. The largest shopping location, **Elias & Co.,** pays tribute to Walt Disney's father, Elias Disney, who was born in Ontario, Canada, and immigrated to California during the Gold Rush.

Mortimer Market is named after the original mouse character that Walt Disney created. He wanted to call it Mortimer Mouse, but his wife, Lillian, encouraged him to change it to Mickey, and the rest is history! Though Mortimer didn't materialize into THE mouse, Mortimer Mouse is a character in the Mickey Mouse animation universe as Mickey's rival for Minnie's affection.

Kingswell Camera Shop pays tribute to Kingswell Avenue, the address of the first office of Walt Disney Studios, where it shared the back of a real estate office.

Atwater Ink and Paint Art Supply pays homage to the significance of the artistry of hand-painted animation. "Ink and Paint" was the name of the animation department of Walt Disney Studios when they drew the outlines and hand-painted the colours of the early Disney films and cartoons. The Atwater Village district of Los Angeles was a regular hangout area for Walt Disney Studio animators.

Fiddler, Fifer & Practical Cafe is a quick service cafe providing Starbucks coffee and quick breakfast and lunch items. The cafe is named after the three pigs and stars of the animated short *The Three Little Pigs* - Fiddler, Fifer, and Practical. The inspiration for the three pigs story and the cafe came from a performing trio made up of Dolly, Dottie, and Ethel, also known as the Silver Lake Sisters, who decided to open up a coffee shop when they retired from their performance careers.

The end of Buena Vista Street is anchored by **Carthay Circle Restaurant,** a lavish and upscale restaurant and two lounges, setting the stage for what is to come in the rest of the park. The Carthay Circle Restaurant is a recreation of Carthay Circle Theatre where Walt Disney first premiered his full-length animated film *Snow White and the Seven Dwarfs* in 1937.

The restaurant is ornate and detailed with treasures and mementos providing a glimpse of the glamorous lifestyle of Old Hollywood. The restaurant includes signature dining experiences, and the Carthay Circle Lounge is the perfect place to enjoy an old- fashioned cocktail.

Club 1901 is a small and exclusive lounge (akin to Club 33 in Disneyland) available only to members and is not open to the public. Club 1901 is a reference to the year 1901 when Walt Disney was born.

Akin to Sleeping Beauty Castle in Disneyland, Carthay Circle serves as the central focal point of Buena Vista Street. While there is a "Partners" statue at Central Hub Plaza in front of the castle, the "Storytellers" statue of Walt Disney and Mickey Mouse together represents the start of a new partnership with the hopes and dreams that Walt Disney arrived in California to achieve.

The **Red Car Trolley** (closed for refurbishment until 2020) is another nostalgic reminder of the energy of Los Angeles in the 1920s and 1930s. Modelled after the Pacific Electric Railway trolleys, this charming and scenic ride takes guests through Buena Vista Street and Hollywood Land. The two cars are the 623 car and the 717 car, historical reminders of when Walt Disney first moved to California (June 1923) and when he first opened Disneyland (July 17, 1955).

20

HOLLYWOOD LAND

DISNEY CALIFORNIA ADVENTURE

Continuing the Golden Age of Hollywood theme, Hollywood Land is a mock studio back lot where the magic of Disney entertainment is celebrated and you can get a behind-the-scenes feel for what it would have been like to be working in a movie studio in the 1930s.

The building across from the Hyperion Theater is modelled after the Walt Disney Studios offices in Glendale, California. Walt Disney was always seen working late at night in his corner office on the third floor, so the third-floor corner office has a light left on as a tribute (similar to the lamp lit in the apartment above the fire station in Disneyland).

Hollywood Land provides a lot of great interactive experiences for young kids and some of the highlights to check out include:

Disney Animation Building

The Disney Animation Building has several different experiences to enjoy and provides a great place to seek refuge from the park for some downtime. It is the perfect place to let little kids nap or run around to burn off extra energy away from the sun and the crowds.

- Animation Academy - Learn step-by-step animation techniques to draw your favourite characters in this interactive, hands-on show from a live Disney animator. Shows run every 30 minutes, featuring different characters throughout the day. Learn to draw one character or you can easily spend several hours learning to draw several different characters with unique souvenirs of your very own personal animation drawings!

- Turtle Talk with Crush - A "totally-tubular" and interactive show with Crush, the turtle from *Finding Nemo*, where he talks directly with the kids in the audience. Each show is unique as he asks questions to the audience and tells stories from his experiences, so it's super fun for the kids and entertaining for the adults (as you're left wondering, *"how do they do that?!"*)

- Sorcerer's Workshop - An interactive experience where you can discover the secrets of animation and enter the Beast's secret library (From *Beauty and the Beast*) to interact with the enchanted book and find out which Disney character you resemble most.

- Anna & Elsa's Royal Welcome - Meet your favourite princess sisters from Arendelle, the Norwegian-inspired kingdom from *Frozen*.

Frozen - Live at the Hyperion

The Hyperion Theater is a nod to the address of the new Walt Disney Studios when they moved in 1926 and is where Mickey Mouse was born. You can watch a live-action theatrical production of the story *Frozen*, with up to five daily shows.

Monsters, Inc. Mike and Sulley to the Rescue

This is a fun attraction where you help Mike and Sulley rescue Boo and return her to her room.

Disney Junior Dance Party!

Another great and interactive show for young kids and preschoolers where they can dance along with all their favourite Disney Junior characters.

Insider tip! Hollywood Land is a great place to visit in the afternoon to get away from the busy crowds and heat. Enjoy all the indoor experiences at the Animation Academy or sit and relax in a quiet environment or take in the Frozen musical for 50 minutes of comfortable seating in an air-conditioned environment.

Guardians of the Galaxy - Mission: BREAKOUT!

Enter the fortress-like museum of the mysterious Collector and join Rocket the Raccoon in a fun rescue of your favourite superheroes from the galaxy! This attraction was reimagined from its predecessor, The Twilight Zone Tower of Terror, and has become a new fan favourite. With more than six different storylines, you can repeat the attraction several times. Experience thrilling free-fall drops in time with music inspired by the movie soundtrack as the Guardians escape and you plunge up and down 13 stories of chaotic mayhem.

Highly recommended must-do fun for thrill-seekers! Guests must be be a minimum of 40 in. (102 cm) tall to ride. This ride is not recommended for pregnant women or anyone with back, neck, or heart problems.

21

CARS LAND

C ars Land opened in 2012 as a part of the billion-dollar overhaul to the park to reinvigorate park goers and present the updated Disney California Adventure Park as a destination and full-day park. Cars Land is a completely immersive experience as soon as you enter the town of Radiator Springs, a life-size replica from the *Cars* films. (And it set the standard for immersive land experiences in subsequent new lands.) Visit "the cutest little town in Carburetor County", a land devoted to Route 66 and California car culture where you can meet the residents of Radiator Springs including Lightning McQueen, Mater, and their car friends.

As **Radiator Springs Racers** is the flagship attraction of Cars Land and one of the most popular attractions, it is one that is not to be missed. It remains just as popular as it was when it opened in 2012! Without FastPasses, the wait times in the standby line often creep up to two hours or more each day during peak times. So it is highly recommended to experience the attraction as early in the day as possible and utilize the Lightning Lane if possible. When the FASTPASS program was available, the FASTPASS options for this attraction were limited and do run out. We have often gone around 1 -2 p.m. in the afternoon and all the FASTPASS for the day were gone.

The ride starts as a scenic drive through the mountains of Ornament Valley. You go through the show building where you head into the town of Radiator Springs, get a race briefing by Doc Hudson, and end with an outdoor side-by-side duelling race to the Comfy Caverns Motor Court.

Guests must be a minimum of 40 in. (102 cm) tall to ride.

Insider tip! The single rider line can be a great option to minimize wait times if you don't "need" to sit together for the ride.

The other two attractions in the land, **Luigi's Rollickin' Roadsters** and **Mater's Junkyard Jamboree** are tame attractions and fun for the little kids.

Must do! Cars Land is the land that brought Disney California Adventure into a new era and the land is unique to Disneyland Resort in California. You don't want to miss Cars Land as it is not in any of the other Disney parks.

Don't miss! See Radiator Springs and Cars Land at night to see the neon signs of the Cozy Cone Motel and Flo Vs's Cafe bringing the area to life.

22

PACIFIC WHARF
DISNEY CALIFORNIA ADVENTURE

The Pacific Wharf area is a charming waterfront destination with a richly themed collection of counter service restaurants with distinctly Californian dining experiences. The atmosphere is themed around the iconic California coastline and the port city feels of Monterey's Cannery Row area and San Francisco's Fisherman's Wharf area. The restaurants in the Pacific Wharf area showcase the rich cultural influences of the ethnically diverse populations of California including the Spanish, Mexican, and Pacific Rim communities that are represented in the culinary options.

Stop by the **Boudin Bakery,** a working replica of the famous bakery that has been delighting San Franciscans for 150 years, to see how the infamous sourdough bread is made. The Bakery Tour gives you an insider look at how the loaves are made. Enjoy samples of fresh bread and then head into the Pacific Wharf Cafe for fresh-made Boudin rolls, sandwiches, and loaves.

Another San Francisco icon is Ghirardelli Chocolates, and the **Ghirardelli Soda Fountain and Chocolate Shop** brings its chocolates for premium sundaes, ice cream cones and milkshake treats.

Enjoy classic Mediterranean and Italian favourites at **Alfresco Tasting Terrace** and **Wine Country Trattoria**, or sample a variety of wines at **Mendocino Terrace**. Enjoy California wines from the exclusive collection, "Disney Family of Wines", featuring eight wineries whose vintners have a personal connection to the Disney.

California craft beers are highlighted at **Sonoma Terrace** or the **Karl Strauss Handcrafted Beer** truck.

Rounding out the rich culinary experiences in the area are Asian-inspired food options at the **Lucky Fortune Cookery** or Mexican favourites at **Cocina Cucamonga Mexican Grill** and **Rita's Baja Blenders**.

Walt Disney Imagineering Blue Sky Cellar

Want to know how it all starts? The Walt Disney Imagineering Blue Sky Cellar provides a behind-the-scenes look at the creative process to see how "blue sky" ideas for new lands and attractions are turned into reality. From the ideas that are brainstormed to the execution and completion, you get to see the fascinating sketches and 3D models of early conception ideas and the journey they go through to become what you see today.

23

PIXAR PIER
DISNEY CALIFORNIA ADVENTURE

Pixar Pier, formerly Paradise Pier, is a newly reimagined land that opened in June 2018 with a new Pixar theme, bringing Pixar characters and their stories to life. The original land of Paradise Pier was an idyllic version of popular California coastal boardwalks such as the Santa Monica Pier and Santa Cruz Beach Boardwalk. The boardwalk was reimagined into a whimsical boardwalk divided into four neighbourhoods - "Incredibles Park, Toy Story Boardwalk, Pixar Promenade, and Inside Out Headquarters"and has fun activities for all ages.

Incredicoaster is a fan favourite as a thrilling, high-speed roller coaster adventure where you are chasing elusive baby Jack-Jack. The roller coaster ride is speedy, exciting and super fun, great for the adventurous!

Jessie's Critter Carousel and the **Inside Out Emotional Whirl wind** are perfect rides for younger kids or those wanting more tame ride experiences.

The **Pixar Pal-A-Round** Ferris wheel attraction replaces Mickey's Fun Wheel but maintains the iconic Mickey face that is synonymous with the Disney California Adventure pier view. Choose from swinging or non-swinging carts depending on your adventure level.

Toy Story Midway Mania! is fun for the whole family as you participate in a 4D midway-style shooting game to compete for the highest score.

Lamplight Lounge is an elegant and fun gastropub with unique signature cocktails and cuisine that you can enjoy while taking in the waterfront view surrounded by Pixar memorabilia.

Insider tip! The lobster nachos is a highly recommended signature dish at this restaurant.

PARADISE GARDENS PARK

DISNEY CALIFORNIA ADVENTURE

Paradise Gardens Park is the area that complements the pier and includes both attractions and entertainment along Paradise Bay. Daily live entertainment is performed on the bandstand in Paradise Gardens, and it then turns into the viewing area for the nighttime spectacular, **World of Color.**

Fun attractions in the area include **The Little Mermaid - Ariel's Undersea Adventures, Silly Symphony Swings, Jumpin' Jellyfish, Golden Zephyr,** and **Goofy's Sky School,** providing family-friendly fun for all ages.

Select attractions in the area close early for World of Color so you will want to enjoy the rides this area earlier in the day.

GRIZZLY PEAK
DISNEY CALIFORNIA ADVENTURE

The Grizzly Peak area is inspired by the natural beauty of California's wilderness, the rugged Sierra Nevada mountain range and its national parks, "Yosemite and Redwood National Parks".

Grizzly River Run is a whitewater rafting romp that sends you splashing down a mountain amid a raging current and unexpected gushing geysers. The eight-person raft drifts along a lazy river as you head up the mountain and into the wild waters; the descent provides an exhilarating wet and wild ride down the river!

Inspired by the legend of Grizzly Peak, the majestic grizzly bear is the symbol of California in the land of towering peaks, giant trees, and thundering waterfalls. According to early folklore, Grizzly Peak was once a giant bear named Oo-soo'-ma-te, whom A-ha-le the Coyote entrusted with the task to protect the mountain and the land. The coyote turned the bear into stone so that people could not drive the bear away. If you listen closely, you may hear the great bear's spirit roaring along the river! As you make your way towards the debarkation point at the end of the ride, make sure you look for the distinctive bear profile at the top of the mountain.

Insider tip! Prepare to get wet on this ride. Locker storage is available next to the 20-foot tall grizzly bear statue marking the entrance into Grizzly River Run. Lockers are available free of charge for the first two hours.

Grizzly Peak Recreation Area was designed to showcase the rugged Sierra Nevada mountain range that runs along California's eastern border. It also celebrates the significant contribution to California's aviation history with an airfield sub-land themed to the late 1950s and early 1960s.

Soarin' Around the World is another fan favourite where you take flight, spread your wings, and explore the greatest wonders of the world. Originally the attraction was "Soarin' Over California" to celebrate the wonders of California, but the attraction was updated in 2016 to feature locations from around the world. Now guests can glide over the majestic Swiss Alps, the real-world inspiration of the Matterhorn Bobsleds; visit polar bears in Greenland; and see elephants marching toward Mount Kilimanjaro. See the great wonders of the world including the Great Wall of China, the Taj Mahal in India, the Great Pyramids in Egypt, and the Eiffel Tower in Paris.

It's easy to forget you are in Disney California Adventure when the wilderness is all around. At the **Redwood Creek Challenge Trail**, adventure is out there for the whole family where you can explore and enjoy a "forest" range of activities. Visit Spirit Cave hidden in the rocks, where you can visit the enchanted cave and discover your mystical spirit animal.

The trail includes a two-acre course where you can hike, climb, slide, and swing through nature with your favourite *Up* characters. Russell and Dug will cheer you along the way with clues to help you earn your wilderness badge. It's easy to miss, located between Grizzly River Run and The Little Mermaid - Ariel's Undersea Adventure. You can stay as long as you want, so it's a great place for kids to burn off extra energy and take some much-needed downtime in a nature camp environment during the day, away from the parks.

The private entrance into Disney's Grand Californian Hotel is also accessible from Grizzly Peak. Guests must have a valid hotel key card to access the entrance into the hotel.

26

AVENGERS CAMPUS
DISNEY CALIFORNIA ADVENTURE

Originally slated to open in summer of 2020, the opening of the new land was delayed due to the pandemic. Now open as of June 2021, the area next to Guardians of the Galaxy, formerly the land "Bug's Life", is Avengers Campus, a place for new recruits to train and become superheroes in their own story based in the Marvel Cinematic Universe (MCU).

Avengers Campus is an immersive superhero-themed land where guests can join the Avengers team to save the world. The experience is based on attracting and recruiting new extraordinary people to join their team across the world, including a sister campus location at Walt Disney Studios Park at Disneyland Paris.

The back story interconnects with the Stark Expo at Hong Kong Disneyland where first Hydra attacks, and then Thanos attacks. The Avengers realize they need help and the Avengers Campus is created in California and Paris to help recruit people to join the team.

Heroic Encounters

Wanna become a Wakanda Warrior? Recruits can train with the Dora Milage to join their elite fleet or engage in different missions with all your favourite Marvel Superheroes who may be wandering around the campus.

Iron Man, Captain America, Black Widow, Ant-Man and The Wasp, , Captain Marvel, Black Panther, Thor, Loki and the Guardians of the Galaxy will be available to greet new recruits in fun new environments.

Explore the mystic arts with Doctor Strange at the **Ancient Sanctum** where you can learn the mysterious secrets and spells needed to ward off villainous foes.

Spider-Man will be swinging around the campus with gravity-defying acrobatics to greet guests to his new attraction!

WEB SLINGERS: A Spider-Man Adventure

Housed at the Worldwide Engineering Brigade, or **WEB headquarters**, Tony Stark assembled a new initiative to attract the brightest minds to create innovative technologies for the next generation of superheroes. Peter Parker and his team demonstrate Spider-Bots, a new invention of robotic sidekicks to assist him to fight foes but things go awry when the Spider-Bots are replicating quickly without any means to stop the process. Guests will join Spider-Man with their 3D glasses and their own WEB Slinger vehicles to help catch the Spider-Bots on the loose!

This is the first of two attractions that will be available in Avengers Campus and utilizes a virtual queue for guests to be able to experience the attraction. Similar to Star Wars: Rise of the Resistance, the virtual queue will be open each day at 7 a.m and 12 p.m. from the Disneyland app.

A second attraction is planned, featuring Black Panther at the Avengers Headquarters. Guests will have the opportunity to board the Quinjet and fly to Wakanda to join T'Challa and the Avengers in a massive battle against Thanos. (No further details about this attraction are available at this time.)

. . .

Tasty treats can be enjoyed at the **Pym Test Kitchen**, a new mobile ordering quick service eatery where you can choose from tiny treats or big bites created with Pym Particles, or the **Pym Tasting Lab**, a bar and lounge area for adults to enjoy drinks. **Shawarma Palace** offers the best donairs after an epic battle and **Terran Treats** gives you out of this world snacks you cannot find anywhere else.

Avengers Campus promises exciting new experiences and adventures for your very own superhero story and will evolve as it grows.

ALL ABOUT EXPERIENCES

27

DOWNTOWN DISNEY DISTRICT

The Downtown Disney District is the area for outdoor shopping, dining, and entertainment that runs between the park plaza entrance and each of the Disneyland hotels. There is no cost to enter the Downtown Disney area, and it provides a central area of reprieve from the parks when the crowd levels and the heat are at their highest during the day and you need a break, or at the end of a long park day. It's a fun and lively place to spend a non-park day while still enjoying the Disney magic all around. The World of Disney and LEGO stores, as well as boutique stores, provide ample shopping opportunities for families and kids.

There are lots of great dining options available including snacks, grab-and-go options, and sit-down restaurant choices. New restaurants in the area include **Splitsville Luxury Lanes** for upscale dining as well as bowling fun, **Ballast Point Brewing Co.** for casual lounge fare, or **Black Tap Craft Burgers & Shakes** for the newest casual dining option with crazy milkshakes. **Catal Restaurant** is a new signature dining restaurant featuring Mediterranean cuisine. **Salt & Straw** and **Sprinkles** round out the selection with delectable ice cream and bakery treats respectively.

Classic favourites include **Taqueria at Tortilla Joe's** for Mexican fare, **Ralph Brennan's Jazz Kitchen** for New Orleans specialties including their infamous beignets, **Naples Ristorante e Bar** and **Napolini Pizzeria** for Italian pizzas, and **Earl of Sandwich** or **La Brea Bakery Cafe** for sandwiches and salads.

At night, Downtown Disney transforms into a lively place to hang out with continuous live entertainment, local artists, and musicians lining the area. The Downtown Disney District is open until 2 a.m. - perfect for those who are looking for nightlife and entertainment after a day at the parks.

For Star Wars fans, **The VOID** in Downtown Disney opened January 2018 to bring the faraway galaxy a little bit closer to home. Here you can experience Star Wars: Secrets of the Empire in a multi- sensory, hyper-reality experience. As a team of four, you work with a stormtrooper to help the Rebellion in this immersive Star Wars experience outside the parks. Guests must be 48 in. (122 cm) or taller and at least 10 years old to visit. Guests under the age of 16 must also have a parent or guardian present to sign the liability waiver.

Disneyland Monorail

The monorail station is also located in Downtown Disney for a quick and convenient access point into Tomorrowland at Disneyland Park. Valid theme park admission is required to enter the monorail as it takes you directly into the park, bypassing the front entrance.

Parking

For guests who are driving to Downtown Disney, parking fees are in effect but can be validated with valid purchases in Downtown Disney. Enjoy three hours of parking with a minimum purchase of $20 from any Downtown Disney business (including quick service restaurants, kiosks, or stores) and up to five hours of parking validation from a Downtown Disney table service restaurant. Staying beyond the initial validation incurs additional costs of $14 per hour, charged in 30-minute increments up to a daily maximum of $56.

(Prices are valid at time of publishing but please check the Disneyland website for updated pricing.)

28

CHARACTERS

Experiencing your child interact with their favourite Disney characters is one of the most magical encounters at Disney! Watching them react in awe and wonder as they greet their favourite characters is one of the main reasons parents take their children to Disney.

But seeing them on the screen vs. alive and well in front of them may or may not yield the magical reaction you anticipated! Each child is different, and some of the characters may seem overwhelming and intimidating up close and personal, and some are downright scary!

Character meet-and-greet opportunities are available throughout the park, with some available at certain times throughout the day. The Disneyland app will show available characters and the estimated wait time for each character.

You are encouraged to get their autographs, interact with them, and take photos with them. Disney PhotoPass Photographers are available to take photos (which you can then access and download if you have MaxPass purchased), but you can also take photos with your phone or camera as well. While the Disney PhotoPass Photographers cannot take photos with your phone or camera, the Cast Member assigned as the "handler" for the character will be able to take a photo with your camera or phone for you.

Where you can find your favourite characters:

There are some areas where you are more likely to find characters for photos and autographs, characters are also known to "roam" around the parks too so just keep your eyes open as you never know who may show up!

Disneyland

- Town Square - different characters throughout the day
- Toontown - Mickey and Minnie Mouse and friends
- Pixie Hollow - Tinkerbell and fairy friends
- Fantasy Faire - Disney Princesses
- Critter Country - Winnie the Pooh and friends
- Star Wars Launch Bay - Star Wars characters such as Darth Vader and Chewbacca (although this may change with the opening of Star Wars: Galaxy's Edge)
- Star Wars: Galaxy's Edge - the land is more of an immersive experience, so there won't be character meet-and-greets, but you may see characters such as Stormtroopers, Rey, and Chewbacca walking through.

Disney California Adventure

- Buena Vista Street - different characters throughout the day
- Hollywood Land - superhero encounters
- Hollywood Land, Animation Building - Anna, Elsa, Olaf
- Hollywood Land, Disney Junior Dance Party - perfect for younger kids; your favourite Disney Junior characters put on a high-energy show with a lively dance party to get the kids dancing and singing along

- Guardians of the Galaxy: Awesome Dance Off - meet Star-Lord, Gamora, and Groot at a fun dance party
- Heroic Encounters at Avengers Campus - Captain America, Iron Man, Spider-Man, Thor, Loki, Dora Milage, Black Panther, Black Widow, Doctor Strange, Ant-Man and The Wasp, Captain Marvel.
- Pixar Pals at Pixar Pier - Woody, Buzz Lightyear, Jessie, the Incredibles Family
- Cars Land - Lightning McQueen, Mater, Red the Fire Engine

New characters are routinely added, so it's always advisable to check the Disneyland app for the most up-to-date information regarding character meet-and-greet opportunities and locations. On different days, you may see some less well-known characters available for photo opportunities and autographs.

Character Dining Meals

Character Dining meals are highly recommended to maximize your character opportunities as you can see several characters in one experience while enjoying a sit-down meal at the same time.

There are five different character meals to choose from, each with different characters and different themes.

At the Parks

For a Character Dining meal inside the park, you can hang out with **Minnie & Friends at Breakfast in the Park** at the **Plaza Inn** at Disneyland. Valid theme park admission is required to dine at the Plaza Inn, a lavish Victorian-themed restaurant serving home-style favourite foods. The Plaza Inn has been a go-to restaurant since its opening. It was designed by Lillian Disney, Walt Disney's wife, who handpicked many of the authentic 19th century furnishings and interior designs. It usually offers the largest selection of characters in one experience as well as creature comfort cuisine.

At Disney Hotels

The other four experiences are located at the Disney hotels. Theme park tickets are not required, nor it is a requirement to be staying at any of the hotels. As such, it is a great option for a non-park day to book a character meal and still enjoy the Disney magic without having to go into the parks.

Goofy's Kitchen at the Disneyland Hotel offers both breakfast and dinner Character Dining meals, with the main Disney characters taking turns coming around to each table to visit with you.

The menu is very kid-friendly with its own kid station at the buffet, and it's also the only place you can find Goofy's peanut butter and jelly pizza and a mac and cheese pizza

Insider tip! Because Goofy's Kitchen is the only restaurant that offers a character meal at dinner, it is especially recommended for your arrival day as an official introduction to your Disney vacation. You have the opportunity to meet all your favourite Disney characters on the first day of your vacation, take photos, get autographs, and get into the Disney vacation mode. Then you can retire early and start your first day at the parks well-rested and eager to explore!

Character Dining experiences are also available at the other two Disney hotels, but they are both breakfast experiences.

Donald Duck's Seaside Breakfast at Disney's **PCH Grill** in the Paradise Pier Hotel is a silly and interactive breakfast where Donald and his friends cause all sorts of mischief during your meal. If you want to see Stitch, then you won't want to miss this breakfast!

Mickey's Tales of Adventure Breakfast Buffet at **Storytellers Cafe** in the Grand Californian Hotel & Spa is a fairly new and higher-end character experience offering both a breakfast buffet (early morning) or brunch buffet (later morning) option with a wide variety of food choices. Mickey and his friends share tales of their recent travel adventures as they make their way through the tables.

The newest Character Dining experience is the most lavish and elaborate, as you will be dining with Disney royalty. The **Disney Princess Breakfast Adventures** at **Napa Rose** in the Grand Californian Hotel & Spa is an unforgettable, one-of-a-kind experience, with a full three- course breakfast and personal visits with all your favourite Disney princesses. This is a high-end princess interactive dining experience and comes with a much higher price tag than the other Character Dining meal options, but it will be the perfect treat for the biggest princess lovers out there!

Advance dining reservations are highly recommended and can be made 60 days in advance. Credit card guarantee is required for reservations, and cancellation penalties apply for cancellations with less than 24 hours' notice, or for no shows. The cancellation or no-show penalty is $10/person for most restaurants, except for the Disney Princess Breakfast experience, which is $25/person. *(Prices are accurate at time of publishing but please check the Disneyland website for updates).*

Prices for the character meals vary between each restaurant. Adult prices are for guests ages 10 and older; children's prices are for kids ages 3 to 9. There is no additional fee for children ages 3 and under.

29

ENTERTAINMENT

The live music and entertainment in the parks is what sets the stage for your magical experience and adds to the atmosphere. Their live stage Broadway-quality shows are top notch and are not to be missed.

Fantasmic!

Frontierland, Disneyland Park

Daring heroes battle epic villains on a grand scale in a jaw-dropping nighttime spectacular starring Mickey Mouse! The Rivers of America are transformed into a canvas for this extravagant live show featuring a fantastical array of live performers, beloved Disney characters, enhanced special effects, and spectacular pyrotechnics, including Maleficent as a 45-foot, fire-breathing dragon!

Seating is available on a first-come-first-serve basis and is available two hours prior to the show. The best spot to watch the show is by the Pirates of the Caribbean attraction, but you will want to get there early. You can also find viewing spots by the Haunted Mansion in New Orleans Square as well.

Insider tip! The second show is not as busy as the early show and recommended if you are staying late at the parks.

A select number of Lighting Lane access options are available to enter a reserved viewing area for guests who want preferred seating.

Fantasmic! dining packages are also available where guests will receive preferred seating vouchers with their meal. Dining packages for Fantasmic! are available with dinner at River Belle Terrace or Blue Bayou Restaurant or with the Fantasmic! On-the-Go Dining Package at Hungry Bear Restaurant.

World of Color

Paradise Gardens Park, Disney California Adventure

If anything, don't miss out on World of Color! This breathtaking extravaganza and outdoor nighttime music spectacular is an experience well worth having. Disney stories are told with a canvas of perfectly timed water jets, movie clips projected with lasers, and pyrotechnics that light up in brilliant colours. Scenes from your favourite Disney and Pixar movies are weaved together through fire, water, light, and music to put on the most amazing kaleidoscope of colour and emotion as you watch in amazement and wonder.

The viewing area is around Paradise Bay and space is available on a first-come-first-serve basis. Lightning Lane access to the show is highly recommended to minimize wait times or else you will need to scope out a good viewing spot a couple of hours before the show.

Lightning Lane access is available for purchase to secure selected viewing areas with a reduced wait time. If you don't want to waste valuable park time saving space for an ideal viewing area for the show, World of Color dining packages are available at select restaurants where you can receive preferred viewing area vouchers to ensure you maximize your show experience.

Reservations for the dining packages are highly recommended, and a credit card is required to guarantee the reservation. There is no penalty to cancel or change your reservation if 24 hours' notice is provided. If you cancel within less than 24 hours of your reservation or decide not to show up, Disney will charge your card a $10/person cancellation or no-show fee. Reservations can be made 60 days in advance.

Each person in your party is required to purchase the dining package to receive a preferred viewing area voucher. The voucher is only valid for the designated showtime and date of the dining experience. Packages are non-refundable, and there is no refund or exchange if shows are cancelled due to weather and/or technical issues.

The viewing area for World of Color, including the preferred viewing area voucher received with a dining package, is standing room only. If you want seating, you can choose to purchase the World of Color Dessert Party tickets to get reserved seating in the preferred viewing area while enjoying a special dessert and a sparkling beverage during the show.

Be a part of the show! Purchase "M**ade with Magic"** accessories that light up and sync to the show for an extra lit, extra magical interactive experience with the show.

Mickey and the Magical Map

Fantasyland, Disneyland Park

Mickey and the Magical Map is a variety show where Mickey takes you to exciting worlds of imagination in a 24-minute performance. With shows running throughout the day, there are plenty of opportunities to enjoy this show where many of your favourite stories come to life in live action and music at the Fantasyland Theatre in Disneyland Park.

Frozen - Live at the Hyperion

Hollywood Land, Disney California Adventure

Experience the emotional and heartwarming story of Anna & Elsa in a spectacular new theatrical interpretation of the animated film *Frozen*. Enjoy the unforgettable story of sister love and the adventures of Olaf, Sven, and Kristoff as they bring Arendelle to life.

Mickey's PhilharMagic

Hollywood Land, Disney California Adventure

Now located at the Sunset Showcase Theater, enjoy this fun 3D fantasy adventure with your beloved Disney characters. Starring Donald Duck, this 12 minute fantasy dream, as we experience his dreams of taking over Mickey's Sorcerer's Hat to conduct the orchestra.

Parades

The parades in Disneyland never get old and are a nice way to break up the day and enjoy some downtime with an upbeat and entertaining break in the parks. Colourful floats, favourite Disney characters, and Disney music provide a fun and energetic pick-me-up in the afternoon. The parade routes run between "it's a small world" and the Town Square promenade. Anywhere along the parade route offers great viewing options, but if you want to snag a park bench or seating along the boulevard for unobstructed views in the front, you will want to find a spot early.

"**Mickey's Soundsational Parade**" was the daily parade in Disneyland running off and on since summer 2011, but it concluded its run on July 17, 2019.

A new parade, "**Magic Happens**" is expected to debut in the spring of 2020. It will celebrate awe-inspiring moments that are the heart of so many Disney stories including new additions from Moana and Coco.

These moments, both large and small, will remind us that we don't need wings to fly, stars to wish upon and magic doesn't stop at midnight.

Minimize your wait time and enjoy a leisurely lunch at the Plaza Inn. With a Plaza Inn Dining Package, you receive a voucher providing exclusive access to the reserved viewing area for the parade in addition to a souvenir lanyard.

There are also seasonal parades that are offered during Christmas and the holidays, and opportunities to see classic favourites such as the "**Main Street Electrical Parade**" and "**Paint the Night Parade**" that may return for limited runs. "Mulan's Lunar New Year Processional" is a seasonal parade in Disney California Adventure that runs in February to celebrate the Lunar New Year along with all the New Year celebrations.

Fireworks at Disneyland Park

Timeless music and appearances by beloved Disney characters accompany a spectacular fireworks show that will leave you enthralled and in awe. Disneyland fireworks are truly a breathtaking experience, and you definitely don't want to miss them!

During peak times (summer and holidays), there may be daily fireworks shows, but in slower seasons, the fireworks shows are usually only on weekends (Friday through Sunday) so you will want to ensure you visit Disneyland on a weekend day if you want to see the fireworks. Fireworks shows are also subject to cancellation in the event of inclement weather, high winds, or lightning. The shows may change during seasons, and there are some that are unique to the season (Fourth of July, Halloween, Christmas holidays, New Year's Eve, etc.).

Recommended viewing locations:

- in front of Sleeping Beauty Castle
- Main Street, U.S.A. between Central Plaza and the Main Street Train Station
- in front of "it's a small world"
- along the Rivers of America in Frontierland

Guests get to be a part of the show with wearable "**Made with Magic"** light-up accessories that are programmed to light up with select parts of the fireworks show.

There are a few other recommended viewing locations such as in Star Wars: Galaxy's Edge or in the esplanade plaza area between the Disneyland Park and Disney California Adventure Park entrances. You won't hear the music or see the visual projections that accompany the fireworks show but you will still get to see the fireworks though.

Guests staying at any of the Disney hotels (Grand Californian, Disneyland Hotel, or Paradise Pier) can also watch the fireworks from the third-floor poolside patio at the Paradise Pier Hotel. Music from the show is played in sync with the fireworks but you won't get to see the visual projections on the castle.

30

DISNEYLAND DINING

Dining at Disneyland can be its own experience, especially for foodies! The level of attention to detail that Walt Disney put into the themed lands is also present in the unique and authentic dining opportunities that complement the overall experience.

Restaurants are generally classified into two categories of service:

- **Table service** (sit-down restaurants, including buffets where you are seated and waited on)
- **Quick service** (where you order your meal at a counter and find your own seating).

Table service and quick service restaurants are available at Disneyland Park, Disney California Adventure Park, Downtown Disney District, and at each of the three Disney hotels: Paradise Pier Hotel, Disneyland Hotel, and Grand Californian Hotel & Spa.

However, unlike Walt Disney World in Orlando, there are no dining plans for Disneyland vacations.

Reservations for table service restaurants and/or Character Dining meals are highly recommended to avoid long wait time to dine, especially during peak times. Without a reservation, guests can easily be waiting over an hour or more to get a table.

Reservations can be made 60 days in advance either online or on the app from your Disney account, or by phoning Disneyland Dining directly at (714) 781-DINE or (714) 781-3463.

A credit card is required at the time of booking the reservation, but nothing will be charged to your card until your reservation date and time.

Changes and cancellations can be made up to 24 hours before reservation time without penalty. Cancellations within less than 24 hours of the reservation time or no shows will be charged $10/person to the credit card on file.

If you are looking for highly recommended restaurant experiences, here are some of the best options to choose from in each park!

Disneyland

Blue Bayou Restaurant

A dining experience unlike any other! The restaurant is located inside the Pirates of the Caribbean attraction, where you sit in an "outdoor" patio under a twilight sky while watching guests go by on boats. It is an intimate and romantic setting along the bayou under a moonlight sky.

Plaza Inn Restaurant

In Main Street, U.S.A., enjoy hearty comfort food classics served in a Victorian-era setting. It is the only restaurant within Disneyland that includes a character breakfast option with Minnie & Friends. The antique charm and decor were designed by Lillian Disney. One of the most popular dishes is the chicken and waffles!

Carnation Cafe

A Main Street, U.S.A. institution, Carnation Cafe is where you go to grab your classic American food favourites at affordable prices, so it's always a popular place to eat. Advance dining reservations are recommended.

The Golden Horseshoe

One of the original restaurants when Disneyland first opened in 1955, The Golden Horseshoe is a Western-style old-time saloon with a spirited live stage show located near the entrance of Frontierland.

The Golden Horseshoe was one of Walt Disney's favourite places to be in the park, and he celebrated his 30th anniversary with his wife, Lillian, with the debut of the original Golden Horseshoe Revue. At one time, it was the "world's longest-running live stage show" according to the *Guinness Book of World Records*.

Now you can enjoy wisecracking jokes and lively Western music with lunch or dinner - hearty grub favourites such as pepper jack chili mac and hand-scooped homemade ice cream and desserts - while reliving the golden age of the western frontier. A U-shaped balcony above the stage is where Walt Disney used to reserve a private box so he could see the show whenever he wanted. Now it is open to the public and anyone can sit there to enjoy their meals and the show.

Reservations are not required as it is considered a quick service restaurant with counter food service and you seat yourself. However, the ambiance is unique, and this restaurant provides you with an indoor break to rest your feet, enjoy the entertainment, and break up your day a bit.

Disney California Adventure

Carthay Circle Restaurant

For an elegant signature dining experience, Carthay Circle Restaurant provides upscale dining cuisine in a recreation of the Carthay Circle Theatre, where Walt Disney first premiered *Snow White and the Seven Dwarfs*, his first full-length animated feature film in 1937. Though there is no dress code to dine there, my nine-year-old definitely noticed that we "were not fancy enough" to be eating there!

Lamplight Lounge is a new addition to the pier, debuting as a part of Pixar Pier. It is a two-story casual waterfront California pub set among the inspiration and creativity of the stories of Pixar. The gastropub lounge is a great place to explore the stories of Pixar with casual pub fare, craft beer, and unique cocktails. The lobster nachos is one of their signature food items.

Wine Country Trattoria

California wines and Italian-inspired cuisine are highlighted at the Wine Country Trattoria for a little Tuscan getaway from the busyness of the parks.

Quick service

Satisfy your hunger with quick and convenient food options at the quick service restaurants when you want to save on valuable park time and you don't want a sit-down meal.

Mobile ordering is available at many of the quick service restaurants, adding a new element of convenience! Browse through menu options within the app, choose your pick up window, place your order, and head straight to the mobile order pick up location to pick it up when you are ready to eat. When you arrive, simply click "I'm Here, Prepare My Order" and the restaurant will begin assembling your order immediately so it is fresh and hot for you when you pick it up.

Where can I drink?

Disneyland Park maintains an innocent, child-like magical space that is fun for all ages. Disney California Adventure Park is like the teenager who is looking for adventure and fun!

Disneyland Park

Until the opening of Star Wars: Galaxy's Edge, there was no place in Disneyland Park that served alcohol. (The only other exception was in **Club 33**, an exclusive member club not accessible to the general public, so it doesn't really count if regular folk like you and me will likely never have the opportunity to visit!) But now, in Star Wars: Galaxy's Edge, **Oga's Cantina** is the first place in Disneyland Park that serves alcoholic beverages. As a remote hangout on the planet Batuu, the drinks are out of this world and unlike any Disneyland experience! Be prepared to wait in line to get in though. It's a small place and highly popular due to its novelty experience, so you may have to wait several hours in line to enter the area. Reservations are highly recommended.

Disney California Adventure

Disney California Adventure is where the grown-ups play - a place where adults can unwind with a well-deserved cocktail, beer, or wine after a long park day.

Carthay Circle Theatre on Buena Vista Street is a great place to unwind and enjoy an upscale dinner in the restaurant upstairs or a glass of wine or spirits in the lounge on the first floor. Step back in time where you feel like you've entered the finest dining establishment in the early 20th century. Kids are not permitted in the lounge area, so the ambiance is perfect for a quiet evening for the adults.

Wine Country Trattoria is a family-friendly restaurant that takes you away from the busyness of the parks into a Tuscan setting, providing you with a temporary break from the theme park environment. With both indoor and outdoor patio seating, the setting provides an intimate and cozy escape with Italian and California-inspired cuisine that pairs perfectly with wine country favourites.

The on-site winery at **Mendocino Terrace** offers wine-tasting from Golden Vine Winery. Craft beer fans can choose from a selection of more than 15 California craft beers at **Sonoma Terrace**.

Lamplight Lounge provides exceptional views of Paradise Bay where you can enjoy unique cocktails or craft beers for a casual and laid-back break.

Over at Avengers Campus, guests can check out **Pym Tasting Lab,** an innovative beverage laboratory and enjoy new specialty craft beers and cocktails made with Pym Particles.

The legal drinking age in California is 21. Valid photo ID is required to purchase alcoholic beverages.

Insider tip! Some places will ask for a passport photo for international guests as an out-of-country driver's license may not accepted as valid photo ID. Take a photo of your passport to store on your smartphone so that you do not have to carry your passport with your in the parks.

Disney Eats and Treats

We just visit for the snacks! There are so many delectable and iconic Disney treats that you can visit Disneyland just for the snacks alone!

DOLE Whip is a popular and iconic Disney treat! This non-dairy soft-serve pineapple-flavoured frozen dessert is always a must-do! It can be found at the Tiki Juice Bar in Adventureland in Disneyland (inside the park) or at Trader Sam's at the Disneyland Hotel (outside the park).

Churros are always another favourite! Don't miss the crispy cinnamon-flavoured fried dough pastry when walking through the park. You may be able to get them in different colours to help celebrate different seasons!

Mickey-shaped beignets in Mint Julep Bar in New Orleans Square or in Cafe Orleans are heaven in a Mickey Mouse shape. Just as good beignets (but just not Mickey-shaped) can be found at Ralph Brennan's Jazz Kitchen Express in Downtown Disney. You'll love the beignets so much you can even buy the beignet powder to take home with you.

Mickey Bars are always a must-do! Decadent creamy ice cream bars in a Mickey-head shape dipped in a thick chocolate are the indulgence that will satisfy your sweet tooth! Ice cream bars will never taste the same after you've enjoyed a Mickey Bar!

Freshly popped buttery popcorn is the perfect snack to accompany your wait for entertainment, and there are plenty of cool and interesting refillable popcorn containers to choose from. The popcorn buckets have become unique souvenir items for many guests, and there is no shortage of creative popcorn buckets to add to your collection.

31

SEASONS

In addition to the year-round fun that Disneyland provides, there are plenty of seasonal celebrations and events to enjoy to add layered experiences, all with a Disney twist and touch to the celebration.

Take note of the following special events that may be happening during your travel dates to complement your trip!

February

Lunar New Year Celebration - Disney California Adventure celebrates the Lunar New Year with multi-cultural Asian traditions and festivities. The characters don traditional Asian attire for vibrant photos in Asian- inspired celebrations.

March

Food & Wine Festival at Disney California Adventure - This popular annual event highlights the food and wine of California featuring dishes and specials from well-known Californian chefs. The festival includes themed kiosks, each highlighting a California-inspired food dish and drink. The event is a must for foodies and includes special events such as culinary demonstrations, spirit seminars, and special appearances.

April

Easter - It's one of the busiest times of the year, so the parks are open earlier and later for the weeks before and after Easter to accommodate the higher crowd levels around that time.

Eggstravaganza - A scavenger hunt for giant specially decorated character eggs hidden throughout both Disneyland Park and Disney California Adventure.

July

Fourth of July - Disneyland is the place to be for the most patriotic of Americans! The parks can be extremely crowded for the day because of its one-of-a-kind Disneyland 4th of July Fireworks celebration that pays tribute to America's history and patriotism. Walt Disney was an extremely patriotic American, and he epitomizes the "American dream" with his story and his legacy. When his older brother, Roy, enlisted in the army for World War I, he wanted to enlist as well but was too young. He ended up forging documents to alter his age to sign up with the American Ambulance Corps, a volunteer group with the Red Cross, to become an ambulance driver in France. He continued his contributions to the war effort in the coming years through his studio's work. Disneyland also continues to offer significant military discounts to military families when they visit the parks.

Many people will go to Disneyland on the 4th of July just for the once-a- year fireworks spectacular and will begin choosing their ideal viewing areas as early as the afternoon! Because of that, the parks begin to get busy around mid-afternoon.

The morning of the day is generally not as busy as most families will have a later start at the parks to stay for the fireworks.

Late September - October

Halloween season at the parks includes fall colour decor and hundreds of hand-carved jack-o'-lanterns throughout Main Street, U.S.A. Characters are dressed in Halloween-themed costumes. Some attractions are re-themed with a Halloween twist, just for the season.

- Haunted Mansion becomes the stage for the Nightmare Before Christmas, hosted by Jack Skellington.
- Space Mountain becomes Space Mountain Ghost Galaxy.
- Guardians of the Galaxy - Mission: BREAKOUT! turns into Guardians of the Galaxy - Monsters After Dark after 5 p.m. for a scary ride.
- Mater's Junkyard Jamboree becomes Mater's Graveyard Jam-BOOree.
- Cars Land celebrates Haul-O-Ween throughout Radiator Springs.

Halloween parties are held on select evenings beginning in mid-September through October for a specially ticketed event where the park is open to those with tickets for the party. The party starts at 7 p.m. and runs through midnight, but guests with a party ticket can enter the parks as early as 4 p.m. to enjoy a few hours in the parks with the general public before the party begins.

In previous years, **Mickey's Not-So-Scary Halloween Party** was held in Disneyland Park on specific nights. In 2019, a new Halloween-themed party was introduced - the **Oogie Boogie Bash** at Disney California Adventure.

The Halloween party requires a separate ticket, but guests will enjoy rare character sightings, hang out with all the classic Disney villains, and go trick-or-treating throughout the park. Specially themed treats and snacks, combined with unique entertainment throughout the night, make for a fun, intimate party with lower crowd levels.

November - December

After Halloween, there is a small time frame before Halloween ends and the parks are transformed into a magical winter wonderland. The Christmas season begins in early to mid-November and runs through the first week of January.

The Town Square Christmas Tree becomes the focal point of the seasonal festivities, while the Sleeping Beauty Castle turns into Sleeping Beauty's Winter Castle, surrounded by icicles and Christmas wreaths and decor, shimmering with twinkling lights for a breathtaking sight.

Certain attractions are transformed as part of the overall holiday season overlay.

- "it's a small world" becomes a World of Holiday magic.
- Haunted Mansion changes to Haunted Mansion Holiday, also known as Haunted Mansion Holiday Nightmare, a continuation of the Nightmare Before Christmas Haunted Mansion version.
- Mater's Junkyard Jamboree becomes Mater's Jingle Jamboree.
- Luigi's Rollickin' Roadsters becomes Luigi's Joy to the Whirl

Special holiday themed entertainment is available during the holiday season including A Christmas Fantasy Parade and a seasonal fireworks show, "Believe....in Holiday Magic".

Thanksgiving at Disneyland is another extremely busy time of year, so advance planning is must if you are visiting over that time. Thanksgiving dinner is a highly coveted experience, but it comes with a steep price tag, and advance dinner reservations are recommended if you want a table service meal anytime during the Thanksgiving weekend.

Other notable celebrations that are recognized in the parks include Kwaanza, Hanukkah, Diwali, and New Year's Eve, although there are no specific celebratory activities devoted to these holidays.

Disneyland After Dark is a series of after-hours ticketed events for guests who want to enjoy a private party atmosphere with specialty themed entertainment, photo ops, and fun food and beverages.

32

VIP TOUR EXPERIENCES

V IP Tour Experiences are available for those who want an elevated and customized Disneyland trip experience or a behind-the-scenes tour with tidbits of history for both Disneyland and Disney California Adventure.

The **Disneyland Resort VIP Tour** is the ultimate VIP theme park experience where you receive your own private Disneyland tour guide and priority access to many of the attractions and shows at the park. You choose what you want to do that day, and your Disney expert guide will share fun behind-the-scenes stories while taking you to the front of the line for the attractions or shows you want to experience. The white-glove service of your personalized tour will ensure you have the most magical day ever with a wealth of premium benefits and experiences you cannot access on your own. Along with the VIP service and your very own personal Disney concierge, you also receive unlimited Disney PhotoPass downloads for the day!

Walk in Walt's Footsteps is a Disneyland tour that takes you through the inspiration, design, and stories of the creation of Disneyland, through Walt Disney's vision, and also includes behind-the-scenes access to some areas not open to the general public, including the

Disneyland Dream Suite in New Orleans Square. This tour is perfect for Disney fans who are fascinated with the man behind the creation of Disneyland, the intricate details of Disneyland, and the inspiration and stories behind each experience in the park.

In Disney California Adventure, the **Disney California Story Tour** provides a peek into California's history at the turn of the century and how it influenced a dreamer like Walt Disney to take the leap to follow his dreams and defy critics to succeed. This tour explores that spirit that inspired the overhaul of the park to experience California as Walt Disney would have experienced it when he first arrived and to delve into the stories behind the icons, attractions, and inspiration.

Available during the holiday season, the "**Holiday Time at the Disneyland Resort Tour**" provides a detailed tour of the magical trans- formation of both parks into the "Merriest Place on Earth". Discover treasured traditions from different areas and enjoy reserved seating for the Christmas Parade and delicious holiday treats, only available during the holiday season.

33

SPECIAL NEEDS

One of the best aspects of spending your vacation time at Disneyland is that it is an inclusive experience for everyone. Disney Cast Members will cater for any special needs or concerns to provide an inclusive experience for each guest. If you have any type of special needs concerns in your family and have been leery of travelling because of it, Disneyland is one of the best places to visit because it is accessible and accommodating.

Physical disabilities

Guests with physical disabilities or mobility issues can enjoy the parks just as much as any able-bodied guest. Guests with wheelchair scooters can bring their own to the parks or rent directly from Disney if preferred.

Both manual wheelchairs and electronic conveyance vehicles (ECVs) can be rented directly from Disney at the Stroller Shop, just outside the entrance to Disneyland Park. This is the only place for rentals and it services both parks. Rentals are available on a first-come-first-serve basis as they cannot be reserved in advance so please arrive early to rent, otherwise, bring your own. Outside companies can also provide rentals as well if needed.

When Disneyland was first opened, it was not originally designed well to accommodate mobility issues, wheelchairs, or ECVs, but many of the attraction queues and facilities have been modified to provide accessibility as much as they can. Disney California Adventure was built in 2001, so they were able to take into account all accessibility issues into the design and layout of the park, so you will notice expansive spaces and larger queue areas to accommodate accessibility.

When entering the parks, head to City Hall in Disneyland Park and/or Chamber of Commerce in Disney California Adventure Park or the Guest Services kiosks to obtain a wheelchair pass.

Disability Access Service (DAS) Pass

The Disability Access Service is a pass available for guests who have a disability that is not necessarily visible and/or prevents them from waiting in a conventional queue environment. The Pass is similar to a virtual wait service that allows you to schedule a return time that is comparable to the current wait time of the attraction so that you are free to enjoy other activities in the park while waiting for the return time to enter the attraction. Similar to FastPass, guests can only hold one attraction return time at any given time. Once that has been used, you can go and obtain a return time for another attraction or ride.

Disney can be very accommodating and will do its best to create an inclusive environment for all needs. Specific needs and concerns can be requested in person at Guest Relations, and a Cast Member will work with you to advise you and provide whatever accessible services you need for your situation.

Allergies

If someone in your family has food allergies, especially life-threatening allergies, it can be a very daunting task to travel as you will always be worried about where and what they can eat. Disney is extremely accommodating for food allergies, intolerances, and dietary and lifestyle requests. This is one of the many reasons why we vacation at Disney as much as we do. For us, it is a safe and accommodating destination.

Menus are available online and in the Disneyland app, so you can review menu items in advance to see if the restaurant has food options to suit your party's needs and preferences. Most restaurants will have allergy-friendly menu items that can accommodate common food allergies, intolerances, and lifestyle requests.

For each table service reservation and meal, Cast Members will ask for any dietary restrictions and allergies at the time of reservation and time of arrival. Guests are encouraged to consult with the chef or a Cast Member trained in special diets who can advise which menu items would be appropriate for the guest. In buffet restaurants, the chef will come out and discuss the food options available that can suit your dietary needs and advise which items should be avoided.

Kosher meals can be accommodated at select restaurants but will require 24 hours' advance notice to accommodate.

Food and non-alcoholic drinks are permitted in the parks, so you can always pack your own if you are concerned about food options and selection, as long as the food or drink containers are not made from glass. Glass is not permitted in the parks and will be confiscated at security.

ALL ABOUT TIPS

34

GOOD TO KNOW

Beyond the basics of what you need to know before your trip, there are lots of little tidbits that can be helpful to know!

Celebrations

Disneyland is the perfect place for any celebration - birthdays, anniversaries, graduations or any kind of milestone. Whatever it is you wish to celebrate at Disneyland, Disney Cast Members want to celebrate it with you! Disneyland offers complimentary celebration buttons for you to personalize and wear throughout the day so Cast Members can recognize your celebration and celebrate with you. Sometimes you may even receive a few extra treats or "pixie dust" because of your celebration button!

Head straight to City Hall in Disneyland or the Chamber of Commerce in Disney California Adventure to pick up your button, or ask for one at any of the stores and they will be happy to personalize a button for you. If it is your first visit to Disneyland, you will want to make sure you obtain a "1st Visit to Disneyland" button. The Cast Members will make you feel so welcome during your first trip! You can also pick up celebration buttons from any store within the parks or at any Disney hotel.

We have been fortunate enough to celebrate both my son's and my daughter's birthdays at Disney World and my 40th birthday at Disneyland in the last few years! We would much rather celebrate with a trip to Disney over buying more stuff, and the memories and experiences of the trip are priceless. They will be forever a part of their childhood memories and that is worth more than anything I could ever buy them.

Reservations 60 days in advance

Reservations for table service restaurants and specialty experiences such as the princess makeovers at Bibbidi Bobbidi Boutique can be made 60 days in advance and are highly recommended.

Credit card information is collected at the time of booking, but nothing will be charged to your card until the reservation time. And you can cancel without penalty up to 24 hours before your reservation date and time. If you wish to cancel or change your reservation, you can do so within the Disneyland app. Any cancellations within 24 hours of the reservation time, may incur a $10 per person cancellation fee. If you don't show up, your card will be charged a $10 per person no-show penalty. If you do need to cancel within 24 hours, it is best to call them directly to cancel and explain your situation, and the restaurant may be able to waive the cancellation fee, but it is not guaranteed.

If you are travelling during peak travel times, reservations at table service restaurants are highly recommended. With higher crowd levels and overall busyness in the parks, a reservation guarantees a sit down dining experience during your trip. Although you may not know exactly when and where you will want to eat during your vacation, it is advisable to book a table service reservation in advance on your park days so that you will have a place to sit down and eat a meal for a nice break. If you decide to "go with the flow" and see what is available, you run the risk of longer wait times if restaurants are fully booked (i.e., over one hour wait times), or eating quick service meals during your trip if no table service restaurants are available when you want to eat.

If you are travelling with young kids, having a table service reservation will ensure you have some built-in sit-downtime to relax and eat and refuel for the next few hours!

We have tried both approaches in the past, and I am always relieved when we have advance reservations so we know when and where we will have some time for a break and a sit-down meal. I am generally more of a "go with the flow" kind of person but that only works at Disneyland when you can be flexible with what, when, and where you want to eat. Because in the middle of the heat, with super crazy busy crowds and long line ups everywhere, you are likely looking for a place indoors with air conditioning, a place to sit down and rest your feet, and decent food menu options. But if you don't have something reserved, what happens is that you look around to see what's available, and it will be a quick service, fast food-type place, with limited seating options.

If there are certain table service restaurants or Character Dining experiences that are a must-do for your trip, then reservations are highly recommended to ensure you get the opportunity to enjoy the experience.

Disneyland mobile app

Download the official **Disneyland** app onto your smartphone to have all the relevant information about Disneyland conveniently at your fingertips. The Disneyland app includes a real-time map of the parks, park hours, entertainment and showtimes, and character meet-and-greet times and locations. It also provides all your dining options, including menu options, pricing, and any allergy or food concerns, and manages all your table service reservations allowing you to add or cancel reservations. Within the app, you are also able to purchase MaxPass and access all your Disney PhotoPass photos.

Insider tip! Make sure you pack a portable battery charger for your phone. Between using the app for mobile ordering, selecting Lightning Lane selections, accessing real-time attraction wait times, character meet locations, taking photos, your smartphone battery will be used up pretty quickly!

Play Disney Parks mobile app

Wait times in line are inevitable at Disneyland, and there will be times when you cannot avoid them. Download the **Play Disney Parks** app (which is different from the official Disneyland app) and explore the parks in a fun and interactive way as you wait in line. The mobile app includes interactive games and experiences that are only available for specific attractions as you are waiting in line. Each attraction has different activities and experiences that are unique to that attraction and are fun for the whole family. There is some fun Disney trivia, and opportunities to earn points. The more you play, the more achievements you earn. It's another extra layer of fun that Disney has added so you don't notice the long wait times!

Single Rider

Many of the most popular rides have Single Rider lines, which is another great option if you are riding alone, or if you don't mind splitting up and not sitting with your travelling party for the ride. As rides fill up and there are spaces remaining, Cast Members will fill up the space with Single Riders to avoid having empty seats. The Single Rider lines move quicker than the regular standby lines, so it's a great choice for repeat experiences if you've already been through it before and want to ride it again! You will just be sitting with other guests rather than your own party.

Rider Switch

Sometimes, parents will face a situation where one child will want to ride a particular attraction, while another cannot (not old enough or not tall enough) or doesn't want to (too scary), so one parent must remain with the other child. Rider Switch allows one parent to ride, and then as soon as the ride is over, the other parent can switch and ride with the child without having to wait in line again. And the lucky child will get to ride twice (once with each parent!).

To stroller or not too stroller? That is the question.

Travelling with young kids often means a stroller is a must. But at what age would you give up on the stroller? Only you will know what your kids will need. A stroller can be very beneficial to have during your Disney days. Going to a theme park means there is a lot of walking. Young kids may not be able to walk as much as you would like, so a stroller is a must if your child needs frequent breaks from walking.

It's also very convenient to store all your stuff in your stroller so you don't have to carry everything with you all the time. You can either bring your own from home or rent one from Disney or one of the third-party companies that specialize in stroller rentals. Please check the Disneyland website for guidelines on maximum stroller dimensions as very large strollers are not permitted in the parks.

However, taking a stroller with you invites a host of limitations and concerns to be aware of. Disneyland is one of the most stroller-congested areas you will encounter and navigating through crowds with a stroller can sometimes be a challenge. Some areas in the parks are just not designed well to accommodate the large number of strollers, so navigation is tricky and frustrating.

You may need to park your stroller outside many rides or when entering buildings. This may be a risk if you leave your belongings in

146 | RENEE TSANG

the stroller. If you leave it unattended, the opportunity is there for your belongings or the stroller to be stolen. So be wary if you decide to bring your expensive stroller to Disneyland.

A Shoe Story

Shoes are probably one of the most important things to consider for your trip. There is going to be a lot of walking, regardless of where you stay. Days are going to be long, so comfortable footwear is key to surviving a Disneyland vacation! Even with the most comfortable shoes, walking all day in them for 10 to 12 hours or more will leave your feet feeling tired and achy. Bring at least two pairs of shoes so that you can alternate between the two to minimize sore feet. Having a change in footwear can offer the break your feet need.

Take breaks throughout the day to rest your feet. Sit-down meals in the middle of the day can offer a nice break. Enjoy some shows or take a ride on the Disneyland Railroad for a nice break.

Photos

Disney PhotoPass Photographers are located in iconic photographic locations throughout the parks to give you memorable Disney vacation photos that have all members of the family in the photo! Access to the photos is available through the Disneyland app. You can receive unlimited downloads of your photos with Disney MaxPass. You can also purchase a one-week PhotoPass plan for one price ($78) to receive unlimited downloads of all your photos up to 45 days after your trip.

Selfie sticks are not permitted in the parks for safety reasons and will be confiscated by security.

Souvenirs

There is no shortage of items you can have as souvenirs! I recommend that you save souvenir purchases until closer to the end of your trip but buy something small on your first day so that the kids are happy with their choice and won't be pestering you for souvenirs during the trip. Then you have the rest of your trip to take the time to look around and decide what you want to purchase.

Autograph books

Make sure each child has their own autograph book to collect the signatures of all their favourite characters at the meet-and-greets.

Lockers

There are lockers available to rent on-site. These are located just outside the main entrance of the parks, inside Disneyland Park on Main Street, U.S.A. (behind the Market House), and inside Disney California Adventure.

Gratuities

Tipping is very much a part of the American culture, and when you are travelling to a new place, it is best to adhere to the traditions and customs of the destination you are visiting. Whether you agree with tipping or not, many of the staff rely on tips as a part of their income, so it's important to recognize that and include tips as a part of your vacation budget.

How much do I tip?

Table service restaurants - 18% - 20% of the pre-tax bill (not including alcoholic beverages) is the norm for table service restaurants, including buffet restaurants. Table service often refers to meals where a server comes to your table to take your order and delivers the food to your table, including buffets where they service your table during your meal. For large parties of six or more (including infants), an automatic 20% gratuity is often added to the bill, so make sure you double-check to see if gratuity is already included or not.

Quick service restaurants - Tips are not required or expected for quick service or counter service restaurants.

Luggage handling - Tips are expected for anyone whether who handles your luggage in your presence whether it be at the airport, at the hotel, or throughout your trip. For bellhops, $1 - $2 per bag is expected or more if it is heavy. For airport transportation, $1 - $2 per bag is expected.

Cab drivers - 15% - 20% is expected.

Housekeeping (a.k.a. mousekeeping) $2 - $5 per night, or $1 - $2 per person, per night as a guideline or more if you make a mess. It is recommended to leave a tip for each day because it may not be the same person cleaning your room each day. It's also recommended to leave a note with your tip to indicate that the money is a tip for housekeeping and not cash you left lying around.

Bar or pool service - $2 - $3 per drink or food order.

Spa and salon services (including Bibbidi Bobbidi Boutique) - 15% - 20% is expected.

Make sure you bring enough cash and small bills to tip all the service staff and Cast Members who aim to make your trip experience worthwhile.

35

PARK STRATEGY

C reating a game plan in advance will help you navigate the parks to ensure you have time to enjoy the must-dos during your trip. Depending on how many days you're visiting the parks, you will likely not be able to experience it all, but you can plan to experience as much as possible during whatever time frame you have for your trip.

Rope Drop

Arrive as soon as the park opens, and take advantage of lower crowd levels to experience the most popular attractions first thing in the morning. There will be little to no wait times on the most popular rides, and you may be able to ride them several times before it gets busy. Then with your favourites already out of the way, you have the rest of the day to enjoy the rest of the park with the option to select Lightning Lane access for whichever rides you want.

As the day goes on, the crowd levels will increase and wait times will get longer. Some of the more popular attractions may also run out of Lightning Lane access early in the day. If you are able to arrive earlier in the day, you have a better chance of riding the most popular attractions and securing any high demand attractions with Lightning Lane access, either individually or through Disney Genie+.

During the peak afternoon time is usually a great time to take a leisurely lunch break, take in the afternoon parades or shows, or even head back to the hotel for a pool break or nap! Afternoon time is when it gets the busiest in the parks, the line ups are the longest, and usually the sun is out in full force, so you will encounter a combination of heat, crowds, hunger, and overstimulation, which is a recipe for meltdowns and disasters!

Magic Morning vs Extra Magic Hour

Staying on-site at a Disney hotel provides you with an Extra Magic Hour so that you can experience the parks one hour before they open to the public each day during your stay. This benefit is only available to guests staying at a Disney hotel, so there will be a lot fewer people in the parks during that early morning hour. This is extremely advantageous for Disney California Adventure as you can go and experience the most popular attractions in the park, including Radiator Springs Racers and Guardians of the Galaxy - Mission: BREAKOUT!, both of which boast long wait times.

If you are staying off-site or at a Good Neighbor hotel, then all tickets purchased in advance with three day or longer admissions will also include *one* Magic Morning access to Disneyland one hour before opening to the general public. Magic Morning can be used on Tuesdays, Thursdays, or Saturdays.

Important to note! Disneyland Park is open one hour earlier on Tuesdays, Thursdays and Saturdays for Magic Morning access for guests who have purchased three day or more tickets in advance, and for Early Magic Hour available to all Disney hotel guests. Disney California Adventure is open one hour earlier on Mondays, Wednesdays, Fridays and Sundays and is only available for Disney hotel guests.

Disney Genie & Disney Genei+

Disney Genie is Disney's virtual vacation planner offering you customized daily park plans, tailored to your preferences. Disney Genie is complimentary and available for all guests to enhance their park plans, offering real-time wait times, forecasted future wait times, mobile ordering access and recommendations on the best times to experience your preferred attractions.

Disney Genie+ is the paid, upgraded option to the complimentary Disney Genie park planner. With Disney Genie, you can pre-select attractions with Lightning Lane access where you can access select attractions in a one-hour window and skip to the front of the line. Spend less time waiting in line, and more time enjoying the park! Once you have used the Lightning Lane access, or the one hour window has passed, you can select your next Lightning Lane attraction.

A limited number of Lightning Lane passes are available for the nighttime spectacular shows (Fantasmic! or World of Color) for each day for preferred viewing locations so you can maximize park time and avoid having to leave early to find a great spot for the nighttime shows. These Lightning Lane passes do not interfere with obtaining attraction Lightning Lane passes.

Breakfast tips

Eat breakfast in your room or at your hotel. Don't waste valuable park time with distractions of food when you first enter the park! Having breakfast in your hotel room before you leave provides you with the fuel to start your day so you can enjoy rides as soon as you get into the parks when wait times are likely shorter. Having no food in your belly and going on adventurous rides can spell nausea and discomfort early in the day, which is no fun!

If you are scheduling a character breakfast, choose a time later in the morning (e.g., 10:30 a.m.) so you can enjoy early morning hours and then take a break when the park starts to get busy as more people arrive.

A park day routine may look a bit different than your usual day at home. Choose quick service meals (and take advantage of mobile ordering for maximum convenience) for quick meals without having to spend too much time on food, stretching out your attraction time for rides and shows.

If you skip the entertainment (afternoon parades, evening shows), these are great opportunities to take advantage of shorter wait times for attractions or restaurant reservations. You might not normally eat lunch at 2 p.m. or 3 p.m., but having a sit-down meal during mid-afternoon allows you to have a hearty meal for the day and enjoy attractions and rides during traditional meal times.

Decisions, decisions!

If you have Extra Magic Hour or Magic Morning with your ticket, then start your day in the park that is hosting the one hour earlier access. Disneyland is open early on Tuesdays, Thursdays, and Saturdays, so if you have access to the early hour, you will want to visit Disneyland on these days.

If you do not have Extra Magic Hour or Magic Morning with your tickets, then you will want to start your day in Disney California Adventure on those days.

Only one day?

If you only have one day to spend at Disneyland, purchase a Park Hopper ticket to access both parks on the same day. Start at Disney California Adventure for the first part of your day, and then head to Disneyland Park for the second half of your day. If you have base ticket and do not want to purchase the Park Hopper option, then I would recommend spending it in Disneyland Park for the day.

Two days

If you have two days to spend at the parks, then 2-day base tickets will give you one full day in each park to fully enjoy the park. Park Hopper tickets are not necessary unless you want the option to go to both parks on the same day.

Three days

If you have 3-day park tickets, then I would suggest spending one day in each park. On the third day, you can either go back to do your favourites in one of the parks or the rides that you missed out on the first two days. If you have base tickets, then I would recommend two days at Disneyland and one day at Disney California Adventure.

Four days

If you have 4-day park tickets, then you have two days to enjoy each park. Spend one day focusing on attractions and the second day for favourites, shows, character meet-and-greets, shopping, and food experiences.

Five days

If you have 5-day park tickets, you can pretty much do it all! You will have lots of time to enjoy everything the park offers at a leisurely pace without having to worry about missing out on anything. You will have time to really soak it all in and appreciate the quality and the level of care and attention in every aspect of the parks.

Must-dos in each park

Here is a list of the must-dos in Disneyland Park:

- Indiana Jones Adventure
- Pirates of the Caribbean
- Haunted Mansion
- Big Thunder Mountain Railroad
- Splash Mountain
- Peter Pan's Flight
- Matterhorn Bobsleds

- "It's a small world"
- Star Tours - The Adventures Continue
- Jungle Cruise
- The Many Adventures of Winnie the Pooh
- Buzz Lightyear Astro Blasters
- Space Mountain
- Fantasmic! A Nighttime Spectacular
- Disneyland Railroad
- Millennium Falcon: Smugglers Run
- Star Wars: Rise of the Resistance (virtual queue)

The Mountain Challenge is a fun challenge where you can receive a special certificate if you conquer all four mountains in one day! (Splash, Space, and Big Thunder Mountain, with the Matterhorn Bobsleds being the fourth mountain.)

If you have young kids, then you will want to make sure you include these attractions and experiences in your trip:

- Mickey's Toontown
- Critter Country including The Many Adventures of Winnie the Pooh and characters
- "it's a small world"
- Jungle Cruise
- Tarzan's Treehouse
- Afternoon parade
- Fantasy Faire including Dumbo the Flying Elephant, Casey Jr. Circus Train, Storybook Land Canal Boats
- Disneyland Railroad

When you first enter Disney California Adventure, make sure you grab a Lightning Lane pass for World of Color if you want to ensure you obtain preferred viewing area access.

Here is a list of the must-dos in Disney California Adventure:

- Radiator Springs Racers
- Guardians of the Galaxy - Mission: BREAKOUT!
- Soarin' Around the World
- Toy Story Midway Mania!
- Grizzly River Run
- Incredicoaster
- WEB SLINGERS: A Spider-Man Adventure (virtual queue)

If you have young kids, then you will want to make sure you enjoy these experiences and attractions:

- Turtle Talk with Crush
- Disney Junior Dance Party
- Redwood Creek Challenge Trail (when you need some downtime)
- Jessie's Critter Carousel
- The Little Mermaid - Ariel's Undersea Adventure
- Cars Land

Disneyland is a park for all ages, and there is something for everyone. But please note the specific requirements for some rides to avoid disappointment. There may be height and/or age requirements that will guide you on which attractions you will be able to experience. Also, having a stroller may restrict your access to some of the attractions as you will have to park the stroller if it's not permitted.

Your children's ages and their interests will be a big guiding factor in how you plan your Disneyland days. As much as you may want to start early and go hard until the park closes, how your child or children react is going to guide your pace and the activities you choose. You may need to stop for naps, stop for a show, skip a show or parade, or go on the same ride over and over again. You may need to leave earlier than you intended or start much later than originally planned. The key is being flexible and listening to your children's needs first to help set the tone and pace of the trip. Hungry, tired, and overstimulated kids will always result in messy meltdowns that can be avoided with proper planning!

Disneyland is much more than the rides. So even if your child is not old enough to enjoy rides, there are so many experiences available that make up the overall experience, so you will never feel like you missed out on anything.

36

TOURING PLAN

It is highly recommended to arrive with some sort of touring plan of how you wish to tackle the parks to maximize your experience and ensure you get to do all the things you want to do. While you do not need to plan out all the details, and there may be some factors outside your control, knowing the lay of the land ahead of time and having a plan regarding your favourite attractions and/or experiences will help you make the most of your time in the parks.

Plan out your park days depending on how many days you plan on spending in each park and what is happening in each park that day.

For first-time visitors, I suggest spending one day in each park to fully experience as much as you can and get comfortable with each park. By your third day, you will have a better idea of both parks, what you enjoyed, what you missed, and what you want to see/do to help guide the next day(s) in the parks.

Find out what your priorities are for the first two days. Decide what type of park day it will be. Will you start early, take a break in the afternoon, and return in the evening? Maybe finish earlier and then return on a different day to stay later for the evening spectacular shows?

Another option is to start a bit later in the day and then go until park closing. This is great for your third and fourth park days where you may need later mornings to get started but will have the stamina to stay later.

Park days can be long, and it can be very exhausting to spend all day in the park from opening to closing, several days in a row. You will need to incorporate some "chill" time to decompress or some non-park days where you can take it a bit easy and not have to worry as much about the schedule for long wait times, parades, and/or showtimes.

I generally recommend starting early on your first day and finishing when you have had enough for the day. End the first day early so you are well-rested for the next few days.

On your second day, start early, but take a break during the afternoon if you need to, and then enjoy the later evening attractions and shows.

The third vacation day is a great day to rest and take a break from the parks. This is a great time to sleep in, enjoy Downtown Disney, or grab a character breakfast at one of the Disney hotels to still enjoy the Disney part of your vacation without having to enter the parks.

Then by the time you get to your third park day (and fourth vacation day), you will be rested enough to start early and end late as best you can to maximize your last day(s) in the parks. I find this works best for most families, but you will know what works best for your family and your kids, and you will be able to gauge that for yourself once you are there.

BASIC TOURING PLAN:

Arrive early. Arrive one hour before park opening, taking into account the time to get through security (and parking if required). If you are planning for the early morning access, arrive about 30 minutes before opening to account for time to get through security.

At 7 a.m., obtain your boarding pass in the Disneyland app to get into the virtual queue for Star Wars: Rise of the Resistance (Disneyland) or WEB SLINGERS: A Spider-Man Adventure (Disney California Adventure). If you are not able to get into the virtual queue at that time, try again at 12 p.m. later that day.

Security. All guests will have to go through security before entering the parks. If you are not taking in a bag, security is a breeze, and you can just walk through. If you do have a bag, then you will need to go through security, and they will search it to ensure you are not bringing in items that are not permitted in the parks.

Food and Snacks. Bringing your own food and snacks is permitted as long as there is no glass. Glass is not permitted in the parks. Hard coolers or loose ice are also not permitted in the parks.

Attractions first. Focus on the most popular attractions for the first few hours. Head to the most popular attractions first to take advantage of lower crowds and shorter wait times. Then you will have plenty of time to enjoy the rest of the park.

Take a break for a late lunch. Head back to the hotel for a break and enjoy the pools or rest/nap if needed.

Return to the park late afternoon for character meets, entertainment, parades, etc. or skip to the attractions and rides if you are not interested in the entertainment.

Enjoy the nighttime entertainment. (Fantasmic! in Disneyland, fireworks show in Disneyland, or World of Color in Disney California Adventure.) The second Fantasmic! Show is not as busy as the first show so you can watch the fireworks from the Frontierland area and then head to the second Fantasmic! Show afterwards.

If you have caught your second wind by now, then the last couple of hours in the park before closing are a great time to enjoy more rides!

Many guests start to leave the parks after the fireworks or evening shows, but Disneyland is usually open for another hour or two, so if you are a night owl, it's a great time to enjoy lower crowd levels and much shorter lines.

37

SAVE, SPLURGE & SOUVENIRS

L et's face it. A trip to Disneyland is going to cost more money than what you may normally spend on vacation. But a Disneyland vacation is a magical experience and likely a bucket list trip for many families, and you will want to save as much as you can but also splurge for certain experiences because they will be worth it!

Find out what's important to your family. What are your family's preferences and priorities so you can decide where you can splurge for the ultimate experience and where you can save.

SAVE

Food - You can bring in your own food, snacks, and drinks into the parks (as long as they're not in glass), so you don't have to purchase all your food in the parks.

Water - Bring your own water bottle and fill up at the fountains or at the quick service restaurants. Water is complimentary at all quick service restaurants.

Quick service meals - These are a convenient option for food as you don't need to pay for gratuities for someone to serve you. Most quick service restaurants can be ordered via the mobile app or can be ordered at the counter for convenience and quick eats.

Breakfast - Find a hotel that includes breakfast. Some of the Good Neighbor Hotels include complimentary breakfast in their rates. If not, grab some breakfast food items to eat in your room before you head for the parks in the morning. Even if your hotel doesn't include complimentary breakfast in their rates, there are many stores in the hotels and area that offer grab and go breakfast items.

Transportation - If you don't need to rent a car, transfers can easily be arranged from the airport to your hotel. Save on car rental fees, gas, and parking fees if you are just staying in the Anaheim area. If you want to have a day or two to explore beyond the Disneyland area, you can always rent a car for a day or two instead of paying for the cost of the whole duration of your trip.

Purchase base tickets - Having the Park Hopper option is extremely convenient but not necessary if you are on a budget and want to trim costs to stretch your dollars further. A 4-day base ticket (one park per day) is cheaper than a 3-day Park Hopper. It gives you two days in each park - lots of time to fully enjoy each park, but removes the convenience of going back and forth on the same day.

SPLURGE

One signature dining experience - Combine it with a nighttime spectacular viewing package to indulge in a signature meal *and* receive preferred access to the nighttime spectacular show (Fantasmic! Or World of Color dining packages).

Character Dining meal - Book Goofy's Kitchen for dinner on your arrival day as the perfect introduction to your Disney vacation! Or book Plaza Inn (late morning reservation) on your Disneyland Park day as theme park admission is required to dine at Plaza Inn. For the other Character Dining meals, booking them on your non-park days is a great way to still get the Disney magic without using a park day.

Bibbidi Bobbidi Boutique - This is a must if you have princesses in your family. What little girl wouldn't want to be pampered and undergo a hair and makeup glam session to turn into a fairy tale princess? It's not just for the girls though, Bibbidi Bobbidi Boutique also has knights packages for little boys too!

Mickey Ears - You absolutely cannot visit the "Happiest Place on Earth" and *not* purchase your own set of Mickey Ears! You can get your Mickey ears embroidered for a unique once-in-a-lifetime souvenir or choose from the many headband styles available.

MaxPass - Purchase MaxPass for everyone in the group when the parks are really crowded, and spend your day doing your favourite must-do attractions to maximize the MaxPass. Save the entertainment, shows, and photos for another day and just do attractions that day. Then on a different day, purchase MaxPass for only one person for the day for the unlimited PhotoPass downloads. Go and find all the Disney PhotoPass characters and photo opportunities to maximize your unlimited downloads option while only purchasing MaxPass for one person.

PhotoPass - A Disney vacation provides unforgettable memories and many opportunities where everyone can be in the photo. Disney PhotoPass Photographers are strategically located in iconic locations in the parks to get you memorable photos from the most iconic moments of your trip. If you do not purchase MaxPass, you can purchase individual photos. You can receive unlimited downloads if you have purchased the one-week PhotoPass.

Disney treats - You have to make room in your budget to indulge in one or two Disney treats at the very least! The problem will be deciding which one! Choose from the iconic Dole Whip, decadent Mickey Bars, Churros, pretzels, or turkey legs to name just a few.

SOUVENIRS

There is no shortage of souvenirs you can purchase in Disneyland to take home with you. And it can take a beating on the pocketbook! From clothing, plush stuffies, toys, jewellery, gadgets, and so much more. But there are some items that fall within the must-have souvenirs for any Disney vacation!

Mickey Ears are a timeless keepsake. You can never have too many! Choose from headbands with ears or the traditional ear hats with the option to personalize the back. Disney continues to offer different styles of the headbands, so you can grow your Mickey headbands collection with each trip.

Pin trading is a fun and unique activity where you can trade pins with Cast Members throughout the park and the Disneyland Resort. Just look at their lanyards and if you see a pin you like, you can trade it with them! Starter sets with a lanyard are available to purchase so you can get started and then you can trade until you are happy with your pin collection! There are even pin-trading events where you can trade with other people until you find the right pins to add to your collection.

Note: Pin collecting and pin trading can be addicting, but the cost of pins can easily add up. Trade genuine and authentic Disney pins to keep the quality and practice respectful. Don't purchase "lots" of pins on eBay as these are usually cheap knock-offs. If you do decide to purchase "lots" of pins in advance, make sure you select a reputable pin seller who can provide you with authentic pins for trading.

Pressed pennies are affordable and fun souvenirs if pin trading is not your thing. It's fun to find and collect pennies to take with you to Disneyland and have them "pressed" into Disneyland souvenirs for a unique collectible. There are machines located throughout the parks with different themes and characters. Store them all together in a collectible pressed penny booklet.

ALL ABOUT TRAVEL

38

BOOKING YOUR VACATION

What is the best way to book a Disney vacation?

Generally, where you will receive the best value is to book your flights, hotel, and park tickets together as one package from a tour operator or travel agency. If you book with a travel agent, you can usually reserve the whole package with a deposit and then make payments towards the vacation how you want. The balance is usually not due until about 45 days before you travel.

Booking through a travel agent allows you to review all the options available to customize your vacation package based on your family's specific needs and preferences. They will have expertise in the area and increased access to resources to help you maximize your options and get the best value. Price is only one factor, but so much of your vacation is dependent on what is important to you - flexibility, amenities, special needs and requests, and so much more.

If you book a vacation package directly with the Walt Disney Travel Company (or through a travel agency that books directly with Disney), you can reserve the package with a $200 deposit, and the balance will be due 30 days before travel. A vacation package booked directly with

Disney can include flights if desired, or you can book flights separately as well if the flights offered through Disney are not ideal.

By booking a Walt Disney Travel Company package, you also receive unique perks and benefits including the following: (benefits can change at any time)

- Exclusive collectible pin, lanyard, and luggage tag (one per person on the reservation)
- One 5" x 7" Disney PhotoPass service or selected attraction photo of your choice (one per package)
- Souvenir tickets with one Magic Morning entry on 3-day or longer tickets
- Complimentary $10 ESPN Zone Fame Card
- Accommodation at a Disney Resort hotel or a Good Neighbor Hotel.

Discounted tickets

There are generally no discounted tickets for 1- or 2-day park tickets. Three day or longer tickets offer great value, including one Magic Morning early entrance admission.

Combining your flight and hotel package with Disney tickets is usually where you will receive the greatest savings overall.

Some websites may offer discounted Disney tickets. Be wary of online booking sites and do not book them if you are not comfortable. Disney sells tickets directly, and through reputable ticket resellers, and travel agencies so make sure you are purchasing tickets through a credible source. Ticket purchases are non-refundable and non-transferable so don't risk losing all your money from a not trustworthy source just to save a few dollars.

BOOKING YOUR VACATION

Airports

Most travellers will fly into Los Angeles International Airport (LAX) as it is the primary international airport servicing Los Angeles and surrounding areas. Anaheim is about an hour south of LAX.

John Wayne Airport, Orange County (SNA) is one of the closest airports to Anaheim and is extremely convenient for Disneyland vacations.

San Diego International Airport (SAN) is about two hours south of Anaheim. A popular option to get to Anaheim is aboard the Amtrak Pacific Surfliner, a two hour train ride along the Southern California coast.

There are also several smaller and regional airports in the area that may also be convenient including Hollywood Burbank Airport (BUR), Long Beach Airport (LGB) and Ontario International Airport (ONT) depending on flight options.

Transportation

Ground transportation to Disneyland Resort is available from LAX and SNA. Shuttle transfers and private transfers are available. The Disneyland Resort Express, although not operated or affiliated with Disney, offers an affordable shuttle service from both LAX and SNA to Disneyland Resort hotels and several Good Neighbor Hotels in Anaheim.

Car seats and booster seats are not required for the Disneyland Resort Express.

If you are staying at one of the Disney hotels or Good Neighbor Hotels in Anaheim and most of your time will be spent at Disneyland, you likely don't have much need for a vehicle. Once you have arrived at your hotel, you likely won't need your car again until you leave. You can avoid the added cost of renting a vehicle and paying for parking each day if you don't have any plans to leave the Anaheim area.

The Anaheim Resort Transit (ART) is a low-cost public transportation system that provides convenient access from Anaheim hotels to many of Anaheim's most common tourist attractions, theme parks, shopping, retail, and entertainment options in the area including the cities of Anaheim, Garden Grove, Buena Park, Costa Mesa, and Orange.

Renting a vehicle offers convenience to get around the area and stop off at groceries stores to pick up supplies and food. Taking snacks and food with you into the parks and eating breakfast in your room before you head out are great ways to save money.

As per California law, children must be in car seats or booster seats until age 8 or until they reach a height of 4 feet 9 inches. If you are renting a vehicle, you will want to make sure you bring your car seats and booster seats from home or rent them from the car rental company. Make sure you request them in advance to ensure they are available when you pick up the rental vehicle.

39

DISNEY VACATION SPECIALISTS

Work with your very own white-glove Disney Travel Advisor to plan and book your Disney vacation!

With the prevalence of online booking sites, many individuals don't always think about reaching out to a travel advisor for travel planning assistance. You might not even realize travel agents still exist in this digital online world where information is available at our fingertips.

But, yes, travel agents still exist and are thriving the face of digital competition!

Many are working as independent consultants for larger agencies, and they are home-based, so you don't necessarily see them as you normally would walking through the mall, past a brick-and-mortar agency.

There is a lot of information available online these days, so it's a great place to start your research. As a result, savvy travellers are accessing information at all times of the day, and many travel advisors have adapted their work model to better service client needs.

Travel agents have evolved so much in that they are not just a transaction booking avenue to get the logistical travel details. They have adapted to the wealth of information available by specializing in niche markets to become travel destination experts, offering personalized service and providing travellers with the best vacation and itinerary planning options available to them.

And for something like a Disney vacation, there are plenty of resources available. And yes, you can search through all the information yourself and ask everyone you know about their own experiences with Disney trips for recommendations and advice. It is all a part of the fun! But with all that information and advice available how do you know where to begin and what information to trust?

I just want to throw in the idea of working with a Disney Vacation Specialist to help you with the specialized knowledge that comes with Disney trips because there is so much more to a Disney vacation than just finding the best flights and hotel and getting discounted tickets.

My hope that is this book can provide you with a lot of the information to help you plan your Disneyland vacation, but I encourage you to reach out to work with a travel advisor to make the most of your trip.

This guide provides you with the "bare necessities" of what you need to know to plan your trip but there is so much more information available beyond what I can include. Support a small business, and let the Disney experts help you make your trip even more magical than it already will be!

Why you should use a travel agent

Expertise

By working with a trusted travel advisor, you have the ability to access someone who books travel and deals with travel questions on a daily basis. All of your most commonly asked questions about Disney and travel can be answered easily and conveniently by your travel advisor.

Network

Your travel advisor will have access to a large travel community. To answer any questions, concerns, or special needs you have, your travel advisor will tap into their community and network for expert advice about anything you need that can help make your experience easier and more memorable.

Experience

Travel advisors are also avid and seasoned travellers and know the ins and outs of travel. They can answer your questions or direct you to the appropriate resources for any travel-related questions, both general and specific to your needs.

Resources

They can tap into resources that consumers simply do not have the same access to so that you can get extra benefits or perks, making your vacation smooth and stress-free.

Time

Travel advisors take the time to get to know your preferences and your specific needs. They do the research to find you the best options so you don't have to filter through unnecessary information that is not relevant to what you need. There is a lot of information out there on the internet, as well as opinions from your friends, colleagues, and acquaintances. So how do you know where to begin?

A trusted travel advisor is your BFF in all things travel! We sift through all the extraneous information so you get the answers to what you need to know and what is relevant for your trip. We partner with you to plan your trip to make it special, and we treat it as our own vacation because we are advocates for all the positive benefits of travelling with your kids. We really just want to make sure you have the most amazing trip possible and want to protect your hard-earned vacation investment of both time and money.

A travel advisor can help manage multiple reservations if you are travelling together in a group or with other families, including travelling with children who are not your own. They are able to advise on travel document requirements for unique situations including single-parent travelling, passport requirements, and entry/exit requirements.

As travellers ourselves, and from working with a variety of clients with differing needs, we understand all the concerns with travel. Why pay more if you don't have to? We want you to have the most amazing experience possible while enjoying the greatest value for your money.

Is it worth the upgrade? Sometimes it is, and sometimes there are tips and tricks we can advise. We can help you navigate through all the options so that you make the best decisions that will suit your family's needs, preferences, and budget to have the best time possible.

Last-minute deals

Sometimes it can be tempting to wait for a last-minute deal to get a great price on your vacation. I totally understand; who wouldn't want to take advantage of a fantastic deal?

But with last-minute deals, it is always space that airlines or hotels are looking to fill, so it's only a great deal if you are flexible and not concerned with any specifics regarding flight options, hotel location, or room requirements.

If you have *any* requirements or concerns, booking early to secure the space at a price you are comfortable with is always a better and safer option than taking a wait-and-see approach with the hope of securing a last-minute deal.

40

TRAVEL INSURANCE & PROTECTION PLANS

After finally pulling the trigger and making the decision to take that trip to Disneyland, the excitement of a confirmed trip is exhilarating and the countdown begins!

But it's also just as important to factor in the not-so-exciting cost of travel insurance into your plans. If you have saved up all your hard-earned money to go on this trip, why wouldn't you want to protect yourself and the trip?

So then, how do you protect that vacation investment?

Protecting your travel investment

Travel insurance is not simply medical insurance during the time you will be away. Travel insurance also includes trip cancellation coverage from the minute you purchase any travel product for your vacation, including flights or a deposit on a vacation package that may be months into the future.

And while we all have the intention to travel, there are so many different factors that come into play from the time of purchase through to the time of travel that can affect your vacation plans. Travel insurance really is more of a vacation protection plan to protect your travel investment, to give you options when unexpected events arise that can impact your vacation plans.

"My credit card has travel insurance coverage."

"I have travel insurance through my work benefits."

These are the two most common misconceptions that people have about travel insurance. They believe that what they have is sufficient.

Only when something unexpected happens do they realize that what they had was not sufficient or appropriate and that there is travel insurance coverage that could have protected them from financial loss.

Credit card coverage

It is true that credit cards offer some sort of travel insurance benefits associated with the card, but you need to read the fine print to find out what this coverage includes. Different cards will have different coverage levels. The higher-end premium credit cards will have a higher level of coverage and inclusions as a premium card benefit. But it is up to you to determine if the credit card coverage is sufficient for your needs.

Some may only cover you for a certain number of days, so if you are travelling for a longer period of time, you will want to make sure you purchase top-up coverage.

Some will stipulate that the coverage is available only if you booked on the card.

Sometimes they will require you to call them prior to receiving any treatment. Or others will require you to pay for all the expenses upfront and then you can apply for reimbursement afterwards.

(But will you be able to pay upfront for a major surgery in another country or afford air ambulance service to bring a family member home?)

Some cards will only cover the cardholder, but what about your family or other members of your group?

It is *extremely* important to confirm what your credit card will cover to ensure that you can make an informed decision regarding travel insurance coverage with your credit card and understand their policies for accessing it.

Coverage through work

Group benefits through your job are also an option to look into, but it will be your responsibility to ensure appropriate coverage.

Most group insurance plans through companies provide bare-bones coverage, because companies don't want to overpay for something that is only a benefit to employees.

(Do you think a company is going to overpay on benefits to their employees on something that may only be used by a select few?)

As a result, you will need to look into their specific travel insurance coverage to find out what they cover, who they cover, how much is covered, and their policies for how to access that coverage.

Most group insurance plans also *do not* include any type of **trip cancellation and/or trip delay** coverage. What if something comes up that impacts your travel plans or prevents you from travelling on your original plans? Are you prepared to lose any non-refundable portions of your trip if unforeseen circumstances arise (e.g., health, weather, personal concerns, job loss, etc.)?

Trip cancellation and trip interruption

Most people only consider the medical costs of travel insurance, but what if something unexpected happens *before* your trip and you can no longer go? Certain travel insurance policies will have trip interruption and trip cancellation insurance to cover your trip costs if something unexpected happens and you can no longer go on your trip or need to make changes to return early.

Trip interruption/cancellation coverage is often overlooked but should be purchased to ensure that you can recoup your costs if unexpected events occur. Purchase your travel insurance within 24 hours of booking your flight to ensure that your costs will be covered if you need to cancel your flight and make sure the plan covers unexpected cancellations as not all policies will include this coverage.

While we have the best of intentions to travel when we book and get caught up in the excitement (*"Nothing is going to stop me from going on this trip!"*), unforeseen events may occur that are completely out of your hands.

- You could lose your job and no longer have the funds to travel.
- You or a family member could suffer a medical accident or injury that prevents you from travelling on your original dates.
- Weather can wreak havoc on the best-laid travel plans and if a hurricane or snowstorm prevents the airplanes from travelling, unfortunately, there is nothing you can do to change that!
- Or maybe you've made it to your destination, but an unexpected event occurs *during* your trip that forces you to interrupt your original plans and return home immediately. Usually, that might be if a close family member gets seriously ill (or passes away) while you are away. You will want to rush home as soon as possible. Travel interruption insurance will help cover all the unexpected costs to get home and to recoup any losses from the unused portion of your trip.

These are not always things that we want think about but it is life and it does happen.

. . .

Medical insurance

If you are leaving the country for any length of time, you need to ensure you have some sort of medical insurance in the unlikely event something happens and you need to access medical services in a foreign country.

For us Canadians, we are fortunate enough to have access to a health care system where we do not have to think about the costs of medical services. But to enter a foreign country without medical insurance is a significant risk and gamble that is not worth the chance.

Perhaps people don't purchase travel medical insurance because they erroneously think that they will be fine. They are healthy and nothing will happen to them.

But accidents happen. Broken bone while enjoying an active experience? You'll need to go to the hospital for immediate attention.

An extreme case of food poisoning or sudden allergic reactions can send you to the hospital even if you didn't want to go.

Travel insurance covers you if unexpected events occur. You don't want to be in a situation where you have to shell out thousands and sometimes hundreds of thousands of dollars to receive the medical attention you require. The cost of having adequate travel insurance coverage before you travel is insignificant compared to the medical costs incurred without insurance.

Every travel insurance provider and policy will have different coverage options. Please read the fine print and review all your options to determine if you have the proper coverage you require for your trip.

Travel insurance is often the most overlooked aspect of travel planning, but it is one of the most important! Your vacation is likely a pretty significant financial investment but to overlook travel insurance will be an even costlier mistake.

Make sure you have adequate travel insurance coverage to protect yourself and your trip. The peace of mind that comes with having appropriate coverage is worth its weight in gold, and hopefully you will never need to use it. But we all know that with the best-laid plans and intentions, unexpected events happen, so it's always wise to have protection plans in place.

41

TRAVEL TIPS

I f you've made it this far and your head is spinning with all the things you need to know and you're worried about taking on this travel adventure with your kids, don't let fear steer you away!

Travelling with your kids is one of the most exciting adventures and best experiences you can provide, so it's always worth the effort and the cost. But it is a lot different than travelling on your own or just with adults. There are so many other little details and factors to consider. Just know help is available to make it as easy for you to navigate these uncharted waters.

Family travel specialists are the experts in helping you travel with kids to make it easy for you and your family. They are familiar with the ins and outs of family travel and the unique needs and challenges for families, and they can help alleviate your concerns and make the process as smooth as possible.

Flying with kids for the first time can be very intimidating. Here are a few tips to make the whole process easier.

FLIGHT TIPS

Change of clothes. Always bring a change of clothes for each member of your family packed in your carry-on. You will never know when accidents can happen, and you will be ever grateful that you can change your clothes in the event of any kind of messy accident involving kids (use your own imagination here...).

Electronic devices. Though screen time and overuse of electronic devices are a concern especially for young kids, it is a great way to occupy time on long flights. Download new apps, movies, and shows that they can play or watch during the flight or in the airport. If you're not a fan of taking the electronic devices route with your kids, then books, colouring books and crayons, or journals are all fantastic choices to occupy your child's time when needed. And there are plenty of Disney-themed options available that provide a perfect start to the Disneyland vacation experience before they even arrive!

Earphones/headphones/earbuds are a must! Kids can watch and play their electronics to their hearts' content without you having to worry about them being a nuisance to other travellers. Plus, your flight may have inflight entertainment for you to enjoy. Bring your own headphones so you don't have to pay for them once onboard.

Bring lots of snacks. Hungry and tired kids are a recipe for disaster in any situation, so extra snacks will help keep them calm and curious, especially if you include new snack items they have never tried before.

Chewing gum. If your child has issues with takeoff and landing, chewing gum may help alleviate pain in their ears. Even if they don't have issues, chewing gum can be an extra "treat" in the travel experience and make flying on an airplane more enjoyable.

Check in early. Airlines permit online check in 24 hours before departure where you can select your seats. If you have not paid in advance to select your seats, checking in early online will help you select the seats that will be most advantageous to your family and ensure you are sitting together, close to bathrooms, exits, etc. ... wherever suits your family's needs the best. Canadian airlines now offer complimentary seat selection at the back of the plane to ensure that families with kids under the age of 12 are seated together.

Packing. Allow kids to pack their own carry-on bags. Let them bring their favourite comfort toy with them on their journey.

Reusable bags. Bring lots of resealable bags as you never know what you may need them for! They are fantastic for storing extra food or snacks when kids are peckish or for collecting all the little toys, crayons, books, and paper that you bring along. They are also great for storing wet or dirty clothes in the event you need to change your clothes. If you have soiled clothes, storing them in resealable bags ensures you have a safe place to store them until you can deal with them properly.

Choose flight times wisely. Each family is different, but I would recommend that finding good flight times when flying with kids is far more important than taking advantage of a cheaper and less desirable flight time. And while you may not always want longer layover times, a longer layover time will give kids the opportunity to stretch their legs and explore a new environment to expend some energy and stimulate their curious minds before the next flight.

TRAVEL TIPS

Take your time. Anything you do with kids just takes longer. So travelling is no different. Just factor in extra time for everything and try not to do too much or do it all at once!

Pre-book as much as you can. Make as many arrangements in advance as possible so you can enjoy your trip when you arrive. It's definitely much easier to "go with the flow" when you are travelling as adults without kids, but you don't want to be "going with the flow" when travelling with children.

Be flexible. While you might have some plans outlined for the day, life with kids always has a lot more unexpected elements that may force you to change your plans, so you will need to be flexible to accommodate. Missing a FASTPASS or a show is not the end of the world. There will be another opportunity, so it's OK to change your plans.

Get the kids involved. Kids love to be involved, so let them help you with planning your trip. What are their favourite characters? Their interests can help you plan out your must-sees and must-dos if you are planning a shorter stay and may not be able to see and do everything.

Tell them in advance so they know what to expect. Disneyland can be a very overwhelming experience. Everything you see, hear, and smell is designed to tap into all your senses. The characters can be very exciting to meet, but it may be very overwhelming and scary for some kids, especially if they do not know what to expect!

Bring a car seat if you are renting a vehicle. Travelling with kids means more stuff you have to pack, so you want to pack the essentials, including car seats. If you are renting a vehicle, you don't always know if you will be guaranteed a car seat when you pick up your vehicle or have confidence in the quality of the car seat either. It can be worth the extra hassle to bring your own to keep your child safe in transit and give you peace of mind.

Bring a stroller. Strollers are handy to have to navigate the airport and so that young kids don't have to walk as much in the parks. They are also a great place to store extra bags. Disneyland has stringent stroller requirements, so if you are planning on bringing a stroller, make sure you check the maximum stroller size requirements to ensure they meet the guidelines to enter. You don't want to bring a large stroller with you and then find out it is too big to be allowed in the parks. If you don't want to bring your own, stroller rentals are available directly from Disneyland and other third-party companies in the area.

CONCLUSION

MY PARTING THOUGHTS

I think Peter Pan had the right idea with never growing up! We take on so many responsibilities as we get older; *why can't we just stay young and never grow old?!*

Disney is more than just a vacation. It's a lifestyle. We are not Disney-crazy or anything like that. But more so than anything, Disney guides our way of life. We take inspiration from Walt Disney himself and his dreams to do the impossible. It amazes me how his life lessons and legacy can impact our lives each day.

Beginning with a simple vision to create happiness and delight, he looked for every opportunity to bring joy to an experience, from the smallest detail to his grandeur vision of Disneyland. With passion, dedication, hard work, and a never-ending spirit to persevere, dreams *really* do come true if you believe.

And that with a simple vision, you *can* inspire people to live the dream and never give up. Not on themselves or their dreams.

Through his stories and his legacy, he has inspired me to choose the way I live my life with my kids, the values I want to instill, and the legacy I want leave:

That family and friends are always important.

To see the good in every person and in every situation and that good always triumphs evil.

And that it's OK to dream and to dream big.

That it's fun to do the impossible.

And to believe. To believe in yourself and to believe in your dreams.

Disney stories include core messages around family, friends, values, and dreams. These stories resonate with the values I wish to instill and are one of the many reasons why we continue to have a little bit of Disney in our daily lives however we can!

I hope that after reading this book, the seeds are planted to inspire you to plan a trip to Disneyland! When you need a little magic in your life, take a trip to "the Happiest Place on Earth." Walking through the Main Street U.S.A. will remind you that all is right with the world and your inner child will thank you!

Disneyland is forever evolving and will never be finished. But it is always a place for comfort and a sense of home. And that is exactly the way it is supposed to be.

I'll never grow up! (And neither should you.)

"Disneyland will never be completed.
It will continue to grow as long
as there is imagination left in the world."
Walt Disney

ABOUT THE AUTHOR

Renee Tsang is a travel professional, travel writer, family travel specialist and Disney vacation planner extraordinaire! She is a self-employed travel advisor who plans and books unforgettable vacations, specializing in family travel and Disney destinations.

As a global ambassador for travel, Renee inspires parents to invest in their family with travel experiences. Travel is the best education a parent can give their child and the experience and memories they gain will be far more valuable than anything money can buy.

Based in Calgary, Alberta, Canada, Renee is mom to 2 hilariously goofy kids who keep her forever young. Between sitting in front of a laptop, or playing chauffeur to her kids, you'll find Renee enjoying a glass of wine while planning their annual research trips to Disney. Because *"life is too short to stay home!"*

www.ReneeTsangTravel.com
www.lifeistooshorttostayhome.com

Manufactured by Amazon.ca
Acheson, AB

13258335R00109